Diploma Educators "Teaching Skills"

Course Details

Effective teaching skills can have a big impact on each individual student in the classroom.

This course begins by introducing you to verbal and non-verbal communication and how to use these tools to stimulate a student's thinking. You will also learn the four main participation structures that guide communication, including their advantages and disadvantages. The lessons will also cover how a teacher uses communication in contrast to how a student uses communication. Next, the course will tackle instructional planning.

You will understand the difference between curriculum frameworks and curriculum guides. Additionally, you will learn how to formulate strong, measurable objectives using cognitive or behavioural approaches as well as how to motivate students using theories of motivation, attribution, interest, and self-efficacy.

You will also learn how to select general learning goals for your students. The educational strategies and behaviour management skills taught in this course will benefit all educators and trainers who want to learn more about effective teaching and classroom management.

Teaching Skills and Strategies

These teaching skills can help tutors create engaging and effective learning experiences for their students. Remember that each student is unique, so it's important to adapt and tailor your teaching strategies to meet their individual needs

ISBN: 9798872216605

Active listening

Remember, active listening is a skill that requires practice and self-awareness. Encourage educators to be patient with themselves as they develop and refine their active listening skills. By incorporating these techniques into their training, educators can become more effective listeners and create a more supportive learning environment for their students.

Techniques for teaching active listening skills

Teaching educators active listening skills can greatly enhance their effectiveness as tutors.

Here are some techniques for teaching active listening skills to educators:

Model Active Listening: Start by modelling active listening yourself. Demonstrate the behaviours and techniques associated with active listening, such as maintaining eye contact, nodding, using verbal and non-verbal cues, and paraphrasing or summarising what the speaker is saying.

Explain the Importance: Help educators understand the significance of active listening in the tutoring context. Discuss how active listening builds rapport, fosters trust, and promotes a positive learning environment. Emphasise how it helps tutors better understand students' needs and facilitates effective communication.

Define Active Listening: Provide a clear definition of active listening, including its key elements and characteristics. Explain that active listening involves fully focusing on the speaker, suspending judgment, and giving undivided attention to what is being said.

Provide Examples: Share examples of active listening in action. Use scenarios or role-plays to demonstrate how active listening can be applied during tutoring sessions. Show the difference between active listening responses (reflective, probing, and empathetic) and passive or distracted listening behaviours.

Engage in Reflective Discussions: Engage educators in reflective discussions about their own listening habits and experiences. Encourage them to share times when they felt truly heard and times when they felt their listening skills could have been improved. Discuss the impact of active listening on their own learning and teaching.

Practice Reflective Listening: Pair educators up and have them engage in reflective listening exercises. Each person takes turns speaking while the other practices active listening. Afterward, they provide feedback to each other on their listening skills and the effectiveness of their responses.

Provide Active Listening Strategies: Introduce specific strategies that promote active listening, such as paraphrasing, asking open-ended questions, providing verbal and non-verbal cues, and using clarifying statements. Discuss when and how to use these strategies effectively.

Role-Play Scenarios: Create role-playing scenarios that involve tutoring situations where active listening is crucial. Ask educators to act out the scenarios and practice applying active listening techniques. Provide feedback and guidance on their performance.

Offer Feedback and Reflection: Continuously provide feedback to educators on their active listening skills. Encourage self-reflection by having them assess their own listening behaviours and identify areas for improvement. Encourage ongoing professional development in this area.

Incorporate Active Listening in Training Materials: Integrate active listening skills into training materials for educators. Provide resources, handouts, and practical tips on how to enhance active listening skills. Encourage them to refer to these materials regularly and implement active listening techniques in their tutoring sessions.

Patience

Teaching educators patience skills is important for tutors as it helps them create a supportive and understanding learning environment. Here are some techniques for teaching patience skills to educators:

Discuss the Importance of Patience: Begin by discussing the significance of patience in the tutoring context. Explain how patience allows tutors to create a safe and supportive space for students to learn and grow. Emphasise that patience helps build trust, foster positive relationships, and encourages perseverance.

Define Patience: Provide a clear definition of patience, highlighting its characteristics and how it relates to tutoring. Explain that patience involves staying calm, maintaining composure, and showing understanding and tolerance even in challenging situations.

Share Examples: Share real-life examples of situations where patience is required in tutoring. Discuss scenarios that tutors commonly encounter, such as working with students who may be struggling, experiencing frustration, or needing extra time to grasp concepts. Illustrate how patience can positively impact these situations.

Foster Self-Awareness: Help educators develop self-awareness regarding their own levels of patience. Encourage them to reflect on times when they felt patient and times when they struggled. Discuss the triggers and emotions associated with impatience and how it can affect the tutoring process.

Practice Mindfulness: Introduce educators to mindfulness techniques that can help cultivate patience. Teach them breathing exercises, visualisation, and mindfulness meditation to help them stay present, calm, and focused during tutoring sessions. Discuss how mindfulness can enhance their ability to respond patiently.

Role-Play Scenarios: Create role-playing scenarios that involve challenging tutoring situations where patience is required. Pair educators and have them practice responding with patience and understanding. Afterward, facilitate a discussion to reflect on their experiences and explore alternative approaches.

Encourage Perspective-Taking: Help educators develop empathy and perspective-taking skills. Encourage them to put themselves in their students' shoes and consider the challenges they might be facing. Discuss how understanding students' perspectives can foster patience and compassion.

Provide Strategies for Managing Frustration: Offer educators practical strategies for managing frustration and maintaining patience. Teach them techniques such as deep breathing, taking breaks, positive self-talk, and reframing challenging situations. Discuss how these strategies can help them stay patient and composed.

By implementing these techniques, tutors can develop and enhance their empathy skills, creating a nurturing and supportive learning environment for their students. Remember to continuously reinforce the importance of empathy and provide ongoing support for tutors' professional growth in this area.

Define Empathy: Begin by providing a clear definition of empathy. Explain that empathy is the ability to understand and share the feelings and perspectives of others without judgment. Highlight that empathy involves active listening, perspective-taking, and showing genuine care and concern.

Model Empathetic Behaviour: Model empathetic behaviour yourself as the instructor. Demonstrate active listening, validate emotions, and show understanding during interactions with tutors. This sets an example for them to follow in their own tutoring sessions.

Encourage Perspective-Taking: Help tutors develop the skill of perspective-taking by asking them to imagine themselves in their students' shoes. Encourage them to consider the challenges and emotions that their students might be experiencing. Discuss how understanding different perspectives can enhance empathy.

Share Personal Stories: Share personal stories or anecdotes that highlight the power of empathy in the tutoring context. Discuss situations where empathy made a significant difference in the learning experience and the relationship between the tutor and student.

Practice Active Listening: Teach tutors the importance of active listening in demonstrating empathy. Provide guidance on how to listen attentively, ask open-ended questions, and provide supportive responses that show understanding and empathy for the students' experiences.

Role-Play Scenarios: Create role-playing scenarios that involve challenging tutoring situations where empathy is required. Have tutors practice responding with empathy and understanding. Afterward, facilitate a discussion to reflect on their experiences and explore alternative empathetic approaches.

Encourage Emotional Awareness: Help tutors develop emotional awareness by encouraging them to identify and understand their own emotions. Discuss how being aware of their own feelings can help them relate to and empathise with the emotions of their students.

Teach Non-Verbal Communication: Explain the importance of non-verbal communication in conveying empathy. Discuss the role of facial expressions, body language, and tone of voice in demonstrating empathy. Provide tips and techniques for using non-verbal cues effectively.

Reflect on Student Experiences: Encourage tutors to reflect on their students' experiences and backgrounds. Discuss the impact of culture, personal history, and socio-economic factors on students' lives. This reflection can help tutors develop a deeper understanding and empathy for their students' circumstances.

Foster a Positive Learning Environment: Create a positive and inclusive learning environment that encourages empathy. Emphasise the importance of respect, kindness, and valuing diverse perspectives. Discuss how these elements contribute to an empathetic tutoring experience.

Promote Self-Care: Discuss the significance of self-care for tutors in maintaining empathy. Explain that taking care of their own well-being allows them to better support their students emotionally. Teach strategies for self-care, such as stress management, setting boundaries, and seeking support when needed.

Encourage Reflection and Growth: Encourage tutors to engage in regular self-reflection to assess their empathy skills. Provide opportunities for them to discuss and share their experiences, challenges, and successes in demonstrating empathy. Encourage ongoing growth and development in this area.

Techniques for teaching educators adaptability skills

By implementing these techniques, educators can enhance their adaptability skills and be better equipped to navigate changes in the educational landscape. Remember to create a supportive and nurturing environment that encourages continuous learning and growth in adaptability.

Teaching educators adaptability skills is essential for them to effectively navigate changing circumstances and provide optimal support to their students. Here are some techniques for teaching adaptability skills to educators:

Explain the Concept: Begin by explaining the concept of adaptability and its importance in the field of education. Discuss how adaptability involves being open to change, adjusting strategies and approaches as needed, and embracing new ideas and technologies.

Share Examples: Share real-life examples of situations where adaptability is crucial in the education context. Discuss scenarios that educators commonly encounter, such as changes in curriculum, technology disruptions, or unexpected challenges. Illustrate how adaptability can positively impact these situations.

Foster a Growth Mind-set: Encourage educators to develop a growth mind-set, which is essential for adaptability. Teach them to view challenges as opportunities for growth, embrace feedback, and approach new situations with a willingness to learn and adapt.

Promote Continuous Learning: Emphasise the importance of continuous learning and professional development. Encourage educators to stay updated with the latest research, instructional strategies, and technological advancements in the field. Provide resources and opportunities for ongoing learning.

Discuss Change Management: Teach educators strategies for effectively managing change. Discuss the stages of change, such as denial, resistance, exploration, and commitment. Help them understand their own reactions to change and provide techniques for navigating through each stage.

Problem-Solving and Critical Thinking: Teach educators problem-solving and critical thinking skills, as these abilities are closely tied to adaptability. Provide opportunities for them to practice analysing situations, identifying alternative solutions, and making informed decisions.

Encourage Collaboration: Foster a collaborative culture among educators. Encourage them to share experiences, strategies, and best practices with their peers. Collaborative discussions can expose educators to different perspectives and innovative approaches, enhancing their adaptability.

Simulate Scenarios: Create simulated scenarios that require educators to adapt to changing situations. These scenarios can include changes in curriculum, student needs, or unexpected events. Allow educators to brainstorm and implement adaptive strategies in a safe and supportive environment.

Reflective Practice: Incorporate reflective practice into professional development activities. Encourage educators to regularly reflect on their teaching practices, successes, challenges, and areas for improvement. Reflective practice enhances self-awareness and encourages adaptability.

Emphasise Resilience: Teach educators strategies for building resilience. Discuss the importance of maintaining a positive mind-set, managing stress, and seeking support when facing challenges. Resilience is closely linked to adaptability and helps educators bounce back from setbacks.

Celebrate Adaptability: Recognise and celebrate instances where educators demonstrate adaptability. Share success stories and examples of how adaptability positively impacted student learning outcomes. This reinforces the importance of adaptability and motivates educators to continue developing this skill.

Provide Support: Offer ongoing support to educators as they develop their adaptability skills. This can include coaching, mentoring, and access to resources that promote adaptability. Encourage educators to seek guidance and collaborate with colleagues when facing new challenges.

Communication Skills

Clear communication skills are crucial for students to effectively express their ideas, understand others, and succeed in various academic and professional settings. Here are some clear communication skills that you can teach students:

By teaching these clear communication skills, students can enhance their ability to express themselves effectively, understand others, and succeed in various personal, academic, and professional contexts. Encourage regular practice and provide opportunities for students to apply these skills in different communication tasks and activities

Articulation: Teach students to express their thoughts and ideas clearly, using appropriate vocabulary and language. Encourage them to practice speaking fluently and confidently.

Active Listening: Emphasise the importance of active listening. Teach students to focus on the speaker, maintain eye contact, and respond appropriately. Encourage them to ask questions for clarification and paraphrase what they've heard.

Non-Verbal Communication: Teach students about non-verbal cues such as body language, facial expressions, and gestures. Help them understand how these cues can enhance or detract from their communication. Encourage them to be aware of their own non-verbal signals and interpret others' cues accurately.

Organisation and Structure: Teach students to Organise their thoughts and ideas in a logical manner. Discuss the importance of using clear introductions, body paragraphs, and conclusions in both written and verbal communication. Provide guidance on creating outlines or frameworks to Organise their ideas effectively.

Clarity and Conciseness: Encourage students to communicate their messages concisely and clearly. Teach them to avoid jargon, unnecessary details, and convoluted sentences. Emphasise the importance of using straightforward language that is easily understood by others.

Empathy and Perspective-Taking: Help students develop empathy and perspective-taking skills. Teach them to consider the needs, feelings, and perspectives of their audience when communicating. Encourage them to tailor their message accordingly to ensure clarity and understanding.

Use of Visual Aids: Teach students how to use visual aids, such as charts, graphs, diagrams, or slides, to support their verbal communication. Guide them in creating visually appealing and informative visual aids that enhance their message.

Adaptability: Emphasise the importance of adaptability in communication. Teach students to adapt their communication style and delivery based on the context, audience, and purpose. Discuss how adjusting their communication approach can improve clarity and effectiveness.

Use of Examples and Analogies: Encourage students to use relevant examples and analogies to clarify complex concepts or ideas. Teach them to draw comparisons and provide concrete illustrations that make their communication more relatable and understandable.

Feedback and Revision: Teach students to seek and provide constructive feedback on their communication skills. Encourage them to revise and improve their communication based on feedback received. Emphasise the iterative nature of effective communication.

Respectful and Inclusive Language: Teach students the importance of using respectful and inclusive language in their communication. Discuss the impact of words and phrases on others and encourage them to use language that promotes a positive and inclusive environment.

Digital Communication Skills: In today's digital age, it's crucial to teach students effective digital communication skills. Discuss email etiquette, online collaboration tools, and appropriate use of social media platforms. Teach them to communicate professionally and respectfully in digital environments.

By teaching these Organisational skills, students can enhance their ability to manage their time, tasks, and resources effectively. Encourage regular practice and provide support and guidance as they develop these skills. These skills will not only benefit them academically but also in other areas of their lives.

Teaching students Organisational skills is crucial for their academic success and overall well-being. Here are some essential Organisational skills you can teach students:

Time Management: Teach students to effectively manage their time by prioritising tasks, setting goals, and creating schedules or planners. Encourage them to allocate time for studying, assignments, extracurricular activities, and personal commitments.

Planning and Goal Setting: Guide students in setting short-term and long-term goals. Teach them how to break down larger tasks into smaller, manageable steps and create action plans to achieve their goals. Encourage them to regularly review and revise their plans as needed.

Task Prioritisation: Teach students how to prioritise tasks based on their urgency and importance. Help them differentiate between tasks that are essential and those that can be postponed. Discuss strategies such as the Eisenhower Matrix (urgent vs. important) to aid in prioritisation.

Note-Taking: Teach effective note-taking techniques to help students capture and Organise information during classes, lectures, and reading assignments. Discuss methods such as Cornell notes, mind maps, or summarising key points to enhance their note-taking skills.

Organisation of Materials: Guide students in developing strategies to keep their physical and digital materials Organised. Teach them to use folders, binders, and digital folders to store and categorise their papers and documents. Encourage regular decluttering and maintenance of their Organisational systems.

Task Breakdown: Teach students how to break down complex tasks into smaller, more manageable parts. Help them identify the specific steps required to complete a task and create a checklist or timeline to track their progress.

Setting Deadlines: Guide students in setting realistic deadlines for their assignments and projects. Teach them the importance of accounting for potential delays or unforeseen circumstances. Encourage them to set deadlines that allow for ample time for revisions and finalising their work.

Digital Organisation: Teach students strategies for Organising their digital files, emails, and online resources. Discuss techniques such as creating folders, using descriptive filenames, and maintaining an Organised inbox. Emphasise the importance of regular digital decluttering.

Use of Planners and Tools: Introduce students to various Organisational tools such as physical planners, digital calendars, task management apps, or online tools. Help them choose tools that suit their preferences and encourage consistent use.

Proactive Communication: Encourage students to communicate proactively with their educators, peers, and parents. Teach them to clarify instructions, seek help when needed, and advocate for themselves in a respectful and timely manner.

Time Estimation: Help students develop the ability to estimate the time required for different tasks. Guide them in breaking down tasks into smaller time intervals and tracking their actual time spent. This helps them better allocate their time in the future.

Reflection and Evaluation: Teach students the importance of reflecting on their Organisational strategies and evaluating their effectiveness. Encourage them to identify what worked well and areas for improvement. This reflection allows them to refine their Organisational skills continuously.

Remember, teaching time management skills requires consistent reinforcement and practice. Encourage students to persevere and be patient with themselves as they develop these skills. By equipping them with effective time management strategies, students can enhance their productivity, reduce stress, and achieve their academic and personal goals

Teaching students time management skills is crucial for their academic success and overall productivity. Here's an approach on what and how to teach students time management skills:

Explain the Importance: Begin by explaining why time management is important. Help students understand that effective time management allows them to complete tasks efficiently, reduce stress, and achieve their goals.

Identify Time Management Challenges: Discuss common time management challenges students face, such as procrastination, lack of prioritisation, or underestimating task durations. Help them recognise these challenges and their impact on their academic performance.

Goal Setting: Teach students how to set realistic short-term and long-term goals. Help them break down larger goals into smaller, manageable tasks. Emphasise the importance of setting SMART goals (Specific, Measurable, Attainable, Relevant, and Time-bound).

Prioritisation: Guide students in prioritising tasks based on urgency and importance. Teach them techniques like the Eisenhower Matrix, where tasks are categorised as Urgent and Important, Important but not Urgent, Urgent but not Important, or Neither Urgent nor Important.

Creating Schedules and Planners: Teach students to create schedules or planners to allocate time for various activities. Show them how to create a weekly or daily plan that includes classes, study time, extracurricular activities, and personal commitments. Emphasise the importance of time blocks for different tasks.

Breaking Down Tasks: Help students break down larger tasks or assignments into smaller, more manageable parts. Teach them to create checklists or to-do lists that outline specific steps required to complete each task. Encourage them to estimate the time needed for each step.

Time Estimation: Teach students how to estimate the time required to complete tasks. Encourage them to track the time spent on activities to develop a better understanding of their time usage. Discuss the concept of Parkinson's Law (work expands to fill the time available) to highlight the importance of setting realistic deadlines.

Overcoming Procrastination: Address the issue of procrastination and teach students strategies to overcome it. Discuss techniques like the Pomodoro Technique (working in focused bursts with short breaks), setting mini-deadlines, or breaking tasks into smaller, more manageable parts to combat procrastination tendencies.

Managing Distractions: Teach students strategies to manage distractions during study or work time. Discuss techniques like creating a distraction-free environment, using website blockers or apps to limit distractions, and practicing self-discipline.

Self-Reflection and Adjustment: Encourage students to reflect on their time management practices regularly. Help them evaluate their schedules, productivity, and identify areas for improvement. Guide them in making adjustments to their plans based on their reflections.

Providing Resources: Share resources such as time management apps, productivity tools, or techniques that students can explore. Introduce them to digital calendars, task management apps, or time tracking tools that can aid in their time management efforts.

Continuous Support and Monitoring: Provide ongoing support and monitoring as students develop their time management skills. Offer guidance, check-ins, and encouragement. Help them troubleshoot challenges and celebrate their progress.

Teaching students creativity skills can help foster their problem-solving abilities, innovation, and critical thinking. Here's an approach on what and how to teach students creativity skills:

By incorporating these strategies, students can develop and enhance their creativity skills. Remember to foster a supportive and encouraging environment where students feel empowered to think creatively and take risks. Encourage them to embrace their unique perspectives and cultivate their creative potential

Create a Positive and Supportive Environment: Establish a classroom environment that encourages creativity, risk-taking, and open-mindedness. Foster a culture where students feel comfortable expressing their ideas and thoughts without fear of judgment.

Define and Discuss Creativity: Begin by explaining what creativity is and why it's important. Discuss how creativity involves generating new and unique ideas, finding innovative solutions, and thinking outside the box.

Encourage Curiosity and Exploration: Foster a sense of curiosity in students by encouraging them to explore diverse topics, ask questions, and seek knowledge. Encourage them to pursue their interests and engage in independent research or projects.

Promote Divergent Thinking: Teach students to think divergently by brainstorming multiple ideas or solutions for a given problem. Encourage them to generate as many ideas as possible without judgment or evaluation. Emphasise the value of quantity over quality during the brainstorming process.

Emphasise Creative Problem-Solving: Guide students in understanding that creativity is not limited to the arts but can be applied to problem-solving across various subjects. Teach them strategies like brainstorming, mind mapping, and thinking through analogies or metaphors to approach challenges from different angles.

Encourage Collaboration: Promote collaborative activities that require students to work together, exchange ideas, and build on each other's creativity. Assign group projects, discussions, or debates that encourage the sharing and blending of diverse perspectives.

Provide Creative Prompts and Challenges: Offer creative prompts or challenges that stimulate students' thinking and imagination. Present open-ended questions, scenarios, or thought-provoking statements to spark their creativity and encourage unique responses.

Incorporate Arts and Expression: Integrate arts, such as visual arts, music, drama, or creative writing, into the curriculum. Provide opportunities for students to express themselves creatively through different mediums. Encourage them to experiment, take risks, and embrace the process of creation.

Foster Reflection and Iteration: Teach students to reflect on their creative processes and projects. Encourage them to evaluate their work, identify strengths and areas for improvement, and iterate on their ideas. Emphasise that creativity is an ongoing process that involves revision and refinement.

Provide Freedom and Autonomy: Allow students the freedom to explore their own interests and passions within the curriculum. Offer choice-based assignments or projects that provide flexibility and autonomy, allowing them to apply their creativity in their preferred areas.

Embrace Failure and Resilience: Help students understand that failure is a natural part of the creative process. Encourage them to embrace mistakes, learn from them, and persevere through setbacks. Teach them the importance of resilience and the value of iterative improvement.

Celebrate and Showcase Creativity: Provide opportunities for students to showcase and celebrate their creative work. Display their projects, Organise exhibitions or presentations, or encourage them to share their creative ideas with the wider community. This validates their efforts and motivates further creative exploration.

Teaching students flexibility skills can help them adapt to change, think critically, and approach challenges with an open mind-set. Here's an approach on what and how to teach students flexibility skills:

By incorporating these strategies, students can develop and enhance their flexibility skills. Encourage a classroom culture that embraces change, values diverse perspectives, and encourages growth. Help students see flexibility as a valuable asset that contributes to their personal growth and success

Introduce the Concept: Begin by explaining the concept of flexibility and its importance in various aspects of life. Discuss how flexibility involves being open to change, adjusting plans when necessary, and embracing new ideas and perspectives.

Highlight Benefits: Discuss the benefits of being flexible, such as improved problem-solving abilities, reduced stress, and enhanced adaptability. Help students understand how flexibility can positively impact their personal and academic lives.

Emphasise Growth Mind-set: Teach students about the importance of adopting a growth mind-set. Explain that a growth mind-set involves believing in one's ability to learn and grow, embracing challenges, and viewing setbacks as opportunities for improvement. Discuss examples of famous individuals who demonstrate a growth mind-set.

Role-Play Scenarios: Create role-playing scenarios that require students to respond flexibly to unexpected or changing situations. These scenarios can involve academic challenges, group work, or social interactions. Encourage students to brainstorm and practice flexible responses in a safe and supportive environment.

Reflect on Personal Experiences: Engage students in reflection exercises where they identify personal experiences where they demonstrated flexibility or faced challenges due to lack of flexibility. Encourage them to share their insights and discuss the impact of flexibility on those situations.

Problem-Solving Strategies: Teach students various problem-solving strategies, such as brainstorming, considering multiple perspectives, and evaluating alternative solutions. Guide them in applying these strategies to different scenarios, emphasising the importance of flexibility in finding effective solutions.

Encourage Open-Mindedness: Foster open-mindedness by encouraging students to consider diverse perspectives, even if they differ from their own. Facilitate discussions where students respectfully listen to and acknowledge different viewpoints. Teach them to challenge their assumptions and be receptive to new ideas.

Practice Decision-Making: Provide opportunities for students to make decisions in a structured and guided setting. Encourage them to consider multiple options, evaluate pros and cons, and make informed choices. Discuss how flexibility plays a role in adapting decisions based on new information or changing circumstances.

Discuss Resilience: Teach students about resilience and how it relates to flexibility. Discuss the importance of bouncing back from setbacks, learning from failures, and maintaining a positive outlook. Help students develop strategies for building resilience and applying flexibility in challenging situations.

Collaboration and Communication: Promote collaboration and effective communication skills to enhance flexibility. Encourage students to work in groups, exchange ideas, and listen actively to their peers. Teach them to adapt their communication styles to different individuals and situations.

Encourage Creative Problem-Solving: Foster creative problem-solving skills by encouraging students to think outside the box and consider unconventional approaches. Provide opportunities for them to explore alternative solutions and encourage them to embrace innovative ideas.

Celebrate and Recognise Flexibility: Acknowledge and celebrate instances when students demonstrate flexibility. Highlight and discuss examples where flexibility led to positive outcomes. This reinforces the value of flexibility and motivates students to further develop this skill.

Teaching positive reinforcement skills to students can help promote positive behaviours, build self-esteem, and foster a supportive learning environment. Here's an approach on how to teach positive reinforcement skills to students:

By teaching positive reinforcement skills, you can help students develop a growth mind-set, reinforce positive behaviours, and create a supportive and encouraging learning environment. Regularly revisit and reinforce these skills, encouraging students to become active participants in reinforcing positive behaviours within the classroom community.

Explain the Concept: Begin by explaining the concept of positive reinforcement to students. Help them understand that positive reinforcement involves recognising and rewarding desired behaviours to encourage their repetition.

Examples and Discussion: Provide examples of positive reinforcement in action. Discuss situations where positive reinforcement has been effective, both in the classroom and in everyday life. Encourage students to share their own experiences of receiving positive reinforcement.

Identify Desired Behaviours: Help students identify specific behaviours that are desirable and aligned with classroom expectations. Collaboratively create a list of behaviours that demonstrate respect, responsibility, cooperation, or any other positive values relevant to the classroom.

Reinforcement Options: Discuss different types of positive reinforcement, such as verbal praise, written recognition, small rewards, or privileges. Explain that positive reinforcement can vary depending on individual preferences and what motivates each student.

Model Positive Reinforcement: Model positive reinforcement by consistently recognising and acknowledging desired behaviours. Provide specific and genuine praise to students when they exhibit the identified behaviours. Show enthusiasm and sincerity in your positive feedback.

Teach Active Observation: Teach students to actively observe their peers' positive behaviours. Encourage them to be attentive and recognise when others demonstrate the desired behaviours. Explain that they can play an active role in reinforcing positive behaviours by acknowledging them.

Practice Positive Reinforcement: Provide opportunities for students to practice positive reinforcement with their peers. Assign group activities or discussions where students can observe and acknowledge each other's positive behaviours. Offer guidance and feedback on their efforts.

Reinforcement Systems: Consider implementing a reinforcement system, such as a token economy or a reward chart, where students earn points or stickers for displaying positive behaviours. Reinforce the idea that rewards should be tied to specific behaviours and consistently applied.

Encourage Self-Reflection: Foster self-reflection in students by having them evaluate their own behaviour. Teach them to recognise and celebrate their own positive actions and achievements. Encourage them to set personal goals for their behaviour and reward themselves for reaching those goals.

Encourage Peer Feedback: Encourage students to provide positive feedback to their peers when they observe desired behaviours. Teach them to give specific and constructive compliments to their classmates. Foster a classroom culture where positive reinforcement is not only given by the teacher but also by peers.

Reinforcement Language: Teach students to use positive and encouraging language when providing feedback or reinforcement. Discuss the impact of positive words and phrases on others. Encourage them to express their appreciation for others' efforts.

Consistency and Fairness: Emphasise the importance of consistency and fairness in applying positive reinforcement. Explain that it is essential to provide reinforcement consistently and equally to all students to maintain a positive and inclusive classroom environment.

Building rapport with others is an important skill for students to develop, as it contributes to positive relationships and effective communication. Here's an approach on how to teach students how to build rapport:

By teaching students how to build rapport, you help them develop important social and communication skills that contribute to positive relationships. Foster a classroom environment that promotes rapport-building, where students feel supported and encouraged to connect with their peers. Encourage them to apply these skills not only in the classroom but also in their everyday interactions

Define Rapport: Begin by explaining what rapport is and its significance in building relationships. Discuss how rapport involves establishing trust, mutual understanding, and a positive connection with others.

Role-Play and Modelling: Model building rapport by demonstrating positive communication and social skills. Use role-plays or skits to showcase examples of effective rapport-building interactions. Highlight behaviours such as active listening, empathy, and respectful communication.

Active Listening: Teach students the importance of active listening in building rapport. Explain how listening attentively, maintaining eye contact, and responding with empathy and interest can help foster connections with others.

Non-Verbal Communication: Discuss the role of non-verbal communication in building rapport. Teach students about body language, facial expressions, and tone of voice. Help them understand how positive non-verbal cues can contribute to building rapport with others.

Empathy and Perspective-Taking: Guide students in developing empathy and perspective-taking skills. Encourage them to consider others' feelings, perspectives, and experiences. Teach them to show genuine interest in others' thoughts and emotions.

Respect and Positive Attitude: Emphasise the importance of respect and a positive attitude in building rapport. Teach students to treat others with kindness, politeness, and acceptance. Encourage them to focus on strengths and offer encouragement to their peers.

Icebreakers and Group Activities: Incorporate icebreakers and group activities that promote interactions and relationship-building. Provide opportunities for students to engage in collaborative tasks, teamwork, or discussions where they can get to know each other better.

Reflective Discussions: Engage students in reflective discussions about the importance of rapport and their experiences with building relationships. Encourage them to share their thoughts, challenges, and successes in establishing connections with others.

Practice Empathetic Communication: Provide scenarios or case studies that require students to practice empathetic communication. Encourage them to put themselves in others' shoes and respond with understanding and compassion. Offer feedback and guidance on their communication skills.

Appreciation and Recognition: Teach students the importance of showing appreciation and recognising others' strengths and contributions. Encourage them to acknowledge and celebrate their peers' achievements, efforts, and positive qualities.

Conflict Resolution Skills: Teach students conflict resolution skills that foster rapport-building. Help them understand how effective communication, active listening, and finding win-win solutions can contribute to resolving conflicts and maintaining positive relationships.

Continuous Practice: Encourage students to continuously practice rapport-building skills in various contexts. Provide opportunities for them to engage in cooperative learning, group projects, and community activities that allow them to apply and refine their rapport-building abilities.

.

Teaching students how to set clear goals is essential for their personal growth, motivation, and achievement. Here's an approach on how to teach students how to go about setting clear goals:

By teaching students how to set clear goals, you empower them to take ownership of their learning and personal growth. Encourage regular reflection, provide support, and celebrate their achievements along the way. These skills will not only benefit them academically but also in other areas of their lives

Explain the Importance of Goal Setting: Begin by explaining why goal setting is important. Discuss how clear goals provide direction, focus, and motivation. Help students understand that setting goals helps them prioritise, plan, and work towards their desired outcomes.

SMART Goals: Introduce the concept of SMART goals. Explain that SMART stands for Specific, Measurable, Attainable, Relevant, and Time-bound. Discuss each component of SMART goals and provide examples to illustrate their application.

Brainstorming and Identifying Goals: Encourage students to brainstorm and identify personal or academic goals they want to achieve. Guide them in thinking about different areas of their lives, such as academic performance, personal growth, extracurricular activities, or relationships.

Specificity: Teach students the importance of setting specific goals. Help them articulate their goals in clear and precise terms. Encourage them to answer the questions: What exactly do they want to achieve? Why is it important to them?

Measurability: Emphasise the importance of setting goals that can be measured or tracked. Teach students to identify specific criteria or indicators to evaluate their progress and success. Help them define what success will look like for each goal.

Attainability: Guide students in setting goals that are challenging yet attainable. Discuss the importance of setting realistic goals that are within their capabilities and resources. Encourage them to consider their strengths, limitations, and the steps needed to reach their goals.

Relevance: Help students determine the relevance and significance of their goals. Discuss how goals should align with their personal values, interests, and aspirations. Encourage them to reflect on why their goals matter to them and how they connect to their overall well-being or future plans.

Time-bound: Teach students to set time frames or deadlines for their goals. Discuss the importance of setting specific target dates to create a sense of urgency and to track progress effectively. Help them break down long-term goals into shorter-term milestones.

Action Planning: Guide students in creating action plans for each goal. Teach them to identify the steps or tasks required to achieve their goals. Encourage them to think about potential obstacles and strategies for overcoming them.

Reflection and Revision: Foster reflection on goals by encouraging students to regularly review and revise them. Teach them to assess their progress, make adjustments if needed, and celebrate milestones along the way. Emphasise that goal setting is an ongoing process.

Visual Representation: Encourage students to visually represent their goals using tools like vision boards, goal trackers, or progress charts. This helps make their goals more tangible and serves as a visual reminder of their aspirations.

Support and Accountability: Provide support and accountability throughout the goal-setting process. Offer guidance, encouragement, and opportunities for students to share their goals with peers or mentors. Encourage them to provide updates on their progress and seek assistance when needed.

Assess student needs

As educators, assessing student needs is crucial for understanding their strengths, challenges, and learning requirements. Here are some approaches you can use to assess student needs:

Initial Surveys or Questionnaires: Administer surveys or questionnaires at the beginning of the school year or semester to gather information about students' interests, learning styles, goals, and any specific needs or concerns they may have. This provides valuable insights into individual students' needs and preferences.

Observations: Observe students during class activities, discussions, and group work to gather information about their engagement, participation, and areas of strength or challenge. Note any behavioural or learning patterns that may indicate specific needs or areas requiring additional support.

Formative Assessments: Use formative assessments throughout the learning process to gather ongoing feedback and assess students' understanding. These can include quizzes, discussions, short assignments, or informal check-ins. Analyse the results to identify areas where students may require additional instruction or support.

Informal Conversations: Engage in informal conversations with students to establish rapport and gather insights into their needs and experiences. Create a safe and supportive environment where students feel comfortable sharing their thoughts, concerns, or areas where they may require assistance.

Individual Conferences: Schedule individual conferences with students to discuss their progress, goals, and any specific needs or challenges they are facing. These one-on-one meetings provide an opportunity for deeper understanding and personalised support.

Work Samples and Projects: Review students' work samples, projects, and assignments to assess their skills, comprehension, and progress. This allows you to identify areas where students may require additional guidance or enrichment.

Peer Feedback and Collaboration: Encourage students to provide feedback to their peers and collaborate on group projects. Observe their interactions and feedback to gain insights into their abilities, communication skills, and areas where they may need support or development.

Parent or Guardian Input: Communicate with parents or guardians to gather information about students' needs, strengths, and any concerns shared by the family. This collaboration allows for a holistic understanding of the student and facilitates targeted support.

Standardised Assessments: Utilise standardised assessments or tests as one of the assessment methods to gain a broader understanding of students' academic performance and identify any potential learning gaps. However, it is important to consider these assessments in conjunction with other assessment methods for a comprehensive understanding of students' needs.

Special Education or Support Services: Collaborate with special education educators, counsellors, or support service providers to gain insights into students who may require additional accommodations or specialised interventions. This collaboration ensures that the diverse needs of all students are addressed effectively.

Reflective Journals or Self-Assessments: Encourage students to engage in reflective activities, such as journaling or self-assessments, where they can reflect on their own learning experiences, strengths, and areas of improvement. This self-reflection provides valuable information about their own perceptions and needs.

Professional Development and Research: Engage in professional development opportunities and stay updated with research and best practices in education to enhance your understanding of assessing student needs. This ongoing learning helps you refine your assessment strategies and adapt them to diverse student populations.

By using these approaches, you can gather valuable information about students' needs, strengths, and areas requiring support. This information allows you to design personalised instruction, provide targeted interventions, and create a supportive learning environment that addresses the diverse needs of your students

Assessment of needs - students

To conduct a thorough assessment of needs for students, you can follow these steps:

1. Gather Background Information: Collect background information about the students, such as their academic records, previous assessments, individual education plans (IEPs), and any relevant documentation or records. This provides a starting point for understanding their learning history and any existing support needs.

2. Communicate with Students: Engage in conversations with the students to understand their perspectives, interests, goals, and any specific challenges they may be facing. Encourage open and honest communication, allowing them to express their thoughts, concerns, and aspirations.

3. Consult Parents or Guardians: Communicate with parents or guardians to gain insights into their observations, concerns, and any information they can provide about their child's needs or learning style. Collaboration with parents is crucial for a comprehensive understanding of the student.

4. Observe Student Behaviour: Observe students in various learning contexts, such as in the classroom, during group activities, or during independent work. Take note of their engagement, participation, social interactions, and any behaviour that may indicate areas of strength or challenge.

5. Review Work Samples and Assessments: Analyse students' work samples, assignments, tests, and assessments to gauge their academic performance, strengths, and areas requiring further support. Look for patterns or trends that can inform your understanding of their needs.

6. Use Formal Assessments: Administer formal assessments or standardised tests as appropriate to gather objective data on students' academic abilities, such as reading levels, math proficiency, or language skills. Consider a range of assessments to obtain a comprehensive view of students' needs.

7. Consider Individual Learning Styles: Assess students' learning styles, preferences, and strengths. Some students may excel in visual learning, while others may prefer auditory or hands-on approaches. Understanding their learning styles can help tailor instructional strategies and interventions accordingly.

8. Collaborate with Colleagues: Engage in collaborative discussions with other educators, specialists, or support staff who work with the students. Their insights and expertise can contribute to a comprehensive understanding of the students' needs and potential strategies for support.

9. Utilise Self-Assessment Tools: Provide students with self-assessment tools, questionnaires, or reflective activities where they can evaluate their own strengths, challenges, and learning preferences. This self-reflection can provide valuable insights into their perceptions of their needs.

10. Consider Cultural and Linguistic Factors: Recognise and consider the cultural and linguistic backgrounds of students when assessing their needs. Cultural and linguistic factors can influence students' learning styles, communication preferences, and overall educational experiences.

11. Document and Organise Findings: Record and Organise the assessment data, observations, and insights gathered for each student. This documentation serves as a reference for future planning, interventions, and discussions with other stakeholders.

12. Regularly Review and Update Assessments: Remember that assessment of student needs is an ongoing process. Regularly review and update assessments as students' needs may change over time. Continuously monitor progress, gather feedback, and revise instructional strategies accordingly.

By following these steps and utilising a combination of assessment methods, you can gain a comprehensive understanding of students' needs, strengths, and challenges. This information helps you tailor your instruction, interventions, and support to meet their individual requirements effectively.

Teaching students differentiate instruction, is important for promoting inclusive classrooms and addressing diverse learning needs. Here's an approach on how to teach students how to differentiate instruction:

1. Explain Differentiation: Begin by explaining the concept of differentiation in simple terms. Help students understand that differentiation involves tailoring instruction to meet the diverse needs, interests, and abilities of individual learners.

2. Discuss Learning Styles: Introduce the concept of learning styles and help students identify their own preferred ways of learning. Discuss visual, auditory, and kinaesthetic learning styles, as well as other factors like multiple intelligences or cognitive strengths.

3. Explore Differentiation Strategies: Present a range of differentiation strategies that can be used to accommodate various learning needs. Examples include providing different reading materials or resources, offering choice in assignments, using flexible grouping, or adjusting the pace of instruction.

4. Analyse Student Profiles: Have students analyse their own learning profiles by reflecting on their strengths, challenges, and preferences. Encourage them to consider their preferred learning style, subjects they find challenging, and areas where they excel.

5. Create Personal Learning Plans: Guide students in creating personal learning plans based on their profiles. Help them identify specific strategies or adaptations that can support their individual learning needs. Encourage them to set goals and outline steps they can take to achieve them.

6. Model Differentiation Strategies: Model differentiation strategies in the classroom by providing examples of how instruction can be adjusted to accommodate different learners. Show students how assignments, assessments, or instructional materials can be modified to meet diverse needs.

7. Peer Collaboration and Support: Foster a collaborative classroom environment where students can work together to support one another's learning. Encourage peer tutoring, group work, or buddy systems where students can exchange knowledge, skills, and support.

8. Encourage Self-Advocacy: Teach students how to advocate for their own learning needs. Help them develop skills to communicate their preferences, challenges, and required support to educators or other educational professionals.

9.   Reflect on Differentiation Experiences: Engage students in reflective discussions or journaling about their experiences with differentiated instruction. Encourage them to identify what worked well for them and areas where further adaptations may be helpful.

10. Promote Empathy and Understanding: Foster empathy and understanding among students by discussing and appreciating different learning styles, abilities, and strengths. Encourage them to embrace diversity and respect one another's unique learning needs.

11. Encourage Feedback: Create opportunities for students to provide feedback on instructional strategies and adaptations. Seek their input on how instruction can be further tailored to meet their individual needs effectively.

12. Collaborate with Educators: Encourage students to collaborate with their educators in identifying and implementing differentiation strategies. Promote open communication between students and educators to ensure that individual needs are met in the classroom.

By teaching students how to differentiate instruction, you empower them to take an active role in their own learning and create a more inclusive and supportive classroom environment. Emphasise that differentiation benefits all learners and helps create a more engaging and effective learning experience for everyone.

Constructive feedback?

Providing students with constructive feedback is essential for their growth, improvement, and motivation. Here's an approach on how educators can provide constructive feedback to students:

1.   Be specific and Objective: When giving feedback, be specific about what the student did well and areas where improvement is needed. Use objective language and provide clear examples or evidence to support your feedback. This helps students understand exactly what they need to work on.

2.   Focus on the Behaviour or Task: Direct your feedback towards the specific behaviour or task rather than the student as a person. This separates the feedback from personal judgment and encourages students to see it as an opportunity for improvement.

3.   Use a Balanced Approach: Provide a balance of positive feedback and areas for improvement. Acknowledge and highlight the strengths and progress students have made while also addressing areas that require further development. This encourages a growth mind-set and motivates students to strive for continuous improvement.

4.   Be Timely: Provide feedback in a timely manner, ideally as close to the performance or completion of the task as possible. This allows students to make connections between the feedback and their work, enhancing their understanding of the areas that need attention.

5.   Offer Specific Suggestions: Along with pointing out areas for improvement, provide specific suggestions or strategies for how students can enhance their skills or address the identified areas. Offer guidance, resources, or additional practice opportunities that can support their growth.

6.   Maintain a Constructive Tone: Use a positive and encouraging tone when delivering feedback. Frame the feedback in a way that communicates support, belief in the student's potential, and a commitment to their progress. Avoid negative or discouraging language that can undermine motivation.

7.   Encourage Self-Reflection: Encourage students to reflect on their own work and performance. Ask questions that prompt self-assessment, such as "What do you think went well? What could you do differently next time?" This helps students take ownership of their learning and fosters metacognitive skills.

8.   Provide Opportunities for Dialogue: Create a safe and open environment where students feel comfortable discussing the feedback they receive. Encourage them to ask questions, seek clarification, or share their perspectives on the feedback. This promotes a collaborative learning atmosphere.

9. Set Goals: Help students set goals based on the feedback they receive. Guide them in setting realistic and achievable goals that address the areas for improvement. Encourage them to track their progress and celebrate milestones along the way.

10. Encourage Peer Feedback: Foster a classroom culture where students provide constructive feedback to their peers. Teach them to offer specific, helpful, and respectful feedback. Peer feedback not only provides an additional perspective but also promotes a sense of collective responsibility for growth.

11. Follow Up and Follow Through: Check in with students periodically to review their progress and provide ongoing support. Recognise their efforts and provide additional guidance or resources as needed. This demonstrates your commitment to their growth and development.

12. Celebrate Growth and Improvement: Celebrate students' progress and achievements as they make improvements based on the feedback received. This reinforces the value of constructive feedback and motivates students to continue their growth journey.

By following these practices, educators can provide constructive feedback that supports students' development, enhances their learning experience, and fosters a growth mind-set. Remember that feedback should be individualised, tailored to the specific needs of each student, and provided in a manner that promotes a positive and supportive learning environment.

Teaching students problem-solving skills is crucial for their academic and personal success. Here's an approach on how to provide students with problem-solving skills:

1. Introduce the Problem-Solving Process: Start by introducing students to a structured problem-solving process, such as the following steps: understanding the problem, generating possible solutions, evaluating options, implementing a solution, and reflecting on the results.

2. Define the Problem: Teach students how to clearly define and understand the problem at hand. Encourage them to analyse the situation, identify key elements, and consider any constraints or limitations.

3. Generate Possible Solutions: Teach students brainstorming techniques to generate a range of potential solutions or approaches to the problem. Encourage them to think creatively and consider multiple perspectives.

4. Evaluate Options: Guide students in evaluating and analysing their generated solutions. Teach them to consider the pros and cons of each option, assess feasibility, and anticipate potential outcomes.

5. Select a Solution: Help students make informed decisions by guiding them in selecting the most appropriate solution. Encourage them to justify their choices based on evidence, logic, or critical thinking.

6. Implement the Solution: Assist students in developing action plans to implement their chosen solution. Break down the steps required and discuss any resources or support they may need.

7. Reflect on the Results: Encourage students to reflect on the outcomes of their problem-solving efforts. Help them assess the effectiveness of their chosen solution, identify lessons learned, and consider any adjustments or improvements for future problem-solving situations.

8. Teach Decision-Making Strategies: Introduce decision-making strategies that support problem-solving, such as listing pros and cons, using decision matrices, or applying logical reasoning. Provide opportunities for students to practice these strategies in different contexts.

9. Scaffold Problem-Solving Activities: Start with simpler problems and gradually increase the complexity as students develop their problem-solving skills. Provide guidance, support, and examples as needed to scaffold their learning.

10. Encourage Collaboration: Foster collaboration and teamwork by assigning group problem-solving tasks. This allows students to learn from one another, share ideas, and work together to find solutions.

11. Real-World Application: Connect problem-solving skills to real-world scenarios and contexts. Discuss how these skills are relevant in various fields, professions, and everyday life situations. Share examples of individuals who have used problem-solving skills to overcome challenges or achieve success.

12. Provide Feedback and Reflection: Offer constructive feedback on students' problem-solving processes and outcomes. Encourage them to reflect on their problem-solving experiences, identify areas for improvement, and set goals for further development.

By incorporating these strategies, you can equip students with problem-solving skills that will serve them well beyond the classroom. Encourage a growth mind-set, perseverance, and a willingness to take risks. By providing opportunities for students to engage in problem-solving activities and nurturing their problem-solving abilities, you help them become confident, resourceful, and effective problem solvers

Critical thinking skills?

Teaching students critical thinking skills is essential for their intellectual development, ability to analyse information, and make reasoned judgments. Here's an approach on how and why to teach students critical thinking skills:

1. Define Critical Thinking: Begin by explaining what critical thinking is and why it is important. Discuss how critical thinking involves analysing, evaluating, and synthesizing information to form well-reasoned judgments or conclusions.

2. Demonstrate Critical Thinking: Model critical thinking skills by explicitly demonstrating the process of analysing information, asking probing questions, and considering different perspectives. Show students how to critically evaluate sources of information, arguments, or evidence.

3. Ask Open-Ended Questions: Encourage students to ask and answer open-ended questions that require deeper thinking and analysis. Foster discussions that promote critical thinking by challenging assumptions, exploring multiple viewpoints, and seeking evidence or logical reasoning.

4. Teach Information Evaluation: Guide students in evaluating the reliability, credibility, and bias of information sources. Teach them how to assess the accuracy and relevance of information, considering the author's expertise, evidence provided, and potential biases or conflicts of interest.

5. Analyse and Interpret Data: Teach students how to analyse and interpret data in various forms, such as charts, graphs, or text. Help them develop skills in identifying trends, patterns, or relationships and drawing logical conclusions based on the data presented.

6. Problem-Solving and Decision-Making: Engage students in problem-solving activities that require critical thinking. Provide opportunities for them to analyse complex problems, consider multiple solutions, evaluate their viability, and make informed decisions based on available information.

7. Reflective Thinking: Foster reflective thinking by encouraging students to think metacognitively about their own thought processes. Encourage them to evaluate their thinking, identify any biases or assumptions, and consider alternative perspectives or solutions.

8. Teach Logical Reasoning: Introduce logical reasoning skills, such as deductive and inductive reasoning, and teach students to apply these principles when analysing arguments or making logical connections between ideas.

9. Provide Real-World Examples: Connect critical thinking skills to real-world examples and scenarios. Discuss how critical thinking is relevant in various contexts, such as media literacy, scientific inquiry, ethical decision-making, or civic engagement.

10. Encourage Independent Thinking: Foster an environment that encourages independent thinking and expression of ideas. Teach students to think critically about the information presented to them and to form their own opinions supported by evidence and sound reasoning.

11. Collaborative Problem-Solving: Promote collaborative problem-solving activities that require students to work together, share ideas, and engage in respectful debate. Encourage them to challenge and support one another's thinking through constructive feedback and evidence-based arguments.

12. Assess and Provide Feedback: Incorporate assessments and provide feedback that assesses students' critical thinking skills. Provide specific feedback on their ability to analyse, evaluate, and synthesize information, as well as their application of logical reasoning.

By teaching students critical thinking skills, you empower them to become independent thinkers, effective problem solvers, and informed decision-makers. Critical thinking skills are valuable across academic disciplines and are crucial for success in the complex, information-rich world they will encounter. Cultivate a classroom culture that encourages curiosity, open-mindedness, and the willingness to engage critically with ideas and information.

Techniques to motivate students?

Motivating students is a crucial aspect of effective teaching. Here are some techniques that educators can use to motivate students:

1. Set Clear Goals and Expectations: Clearly communicate learning goals and expectations to students. When students understand what is expected of them and what they are working towards, they are more motivated to achieve those goals.

2. Create a Positive Learning Environment: Foster a positive and supportive classroom environment where students feel valued, respected, and safe. Encourage collaboration, active participation, and open communication. Celebrate students' achievements and create opportunities for them to recognise and appreciate their own progress.

3. Use Varied Instructional Strategies: Incorporate a variety of instructional strategies to keep students engaged and motivated. Use a combination of lectures, discussions, hands-on activities, group work, multimedia resources, and technology tools. Differentiate instruction to meet the diverse needs and interests of students.

4. Provide Authentic and Relevant Learning Experiences: Connect learning to real-life situations and students' interests. Help them see the relevance and applicability of what they are learning. Engage students by using examples, case studies, or projects that reflect their experiences and connect to their future goals.

5. Offer Choice and Autonomy: Provide students with choices within the learning process. Offer options for topics, assignments, or modes of assessment to accommodate their interests and preferences. Giving students a sense of autonomy can increase their motivation and ownership of their learning.

6. Set Achievable Challenges: Assign tasks and projects that are appropriately challenging but achievable. When students feel a sense of challenge, they are motivated to apply effort and engage in problem-solving. Provide support and scaffold learning as needed to help students reach the desired level of challenge.

7. Foster Collaboration and Peer Support: Encourage collaboration and cooperative learning activities where students can work together, share ideas, and learn from one another. Foster a classroom culture where students support and motivate each other, building a sense of community and shared learning.

8. Provide Constructive Feedback: Offer timely and specific feedback that focuses on students' efforts, progress, and areas for improvement. Highlight their strengths and provide guidance on how they can further develop their skills. Encourage self-reflection and goal-setting based on the feedback received.

9. Use Gamification or Rewards: Incorporate elements of gamification or rewards to make learning more enjoyable and engaging. Use points, badges, or tangible rewards to recognise students' achievements and progress. Ensure that rewards are tied to effort, growth, or mastery of skills rather than solely focusing on performance outcomes.

10. Tap into Students' Interests and Passions: Explore students' interests, hobbies, or passions and incorporate them into the learning experience. Incorporate relevant examples, case studies, or projects that align with their interests. When students see connections between their interests and the curriculum, they are more motivated to learn.

11. Provide Opportunities for Reflection and Goal-Setting: Engage students in reflection activities where they can evaluate their progress, identify areas for growth, and set personal goals. Encourage them to monitor their own learning and celebrate milestones along the way.

12. Develop Relationships and Show Care: Build positive relationships with your students and show genuine care for their well-being and success. Get to know them individually, listen to their concerns, and offer support when needed. When students feel valued and supported, they are more motivated to engage in the learning process.

Remember that every student is unique, and different motivational techniques may work for different individuals. Be flexible, responsive, and adaptive in your approach, tailoring strategies to meet the specific needs and interests of your students

Building students' confidence is crucial for their academic success and overall well-being. Here are some techniques and skills that educators can use to build students' confidence:

1. Provide Positive and Specific Feedback: Offer frequent and specific positive feedback to students. Acknowledge their efforts, progress, and achievements. Highlight specific strengths and areas of improvement to help them see their growth and build confidence in their abilities.

2. Set Attainable Goals: Set realistic and attainable goals for students. Break down larger tasks into smaller, manageable steps. Celebrate their accomplishments as they achieve these goals, reinforcing their belief in their abilities.

3. Encourage Effort and Persistence: Emphasise the value of effort and hard work. Encourage students to persevere through challenges and setbacks. Help them understand that setbacks are opportunities for growth and learning.

4. Create a Safe and Supportive Environment: Foster a classroom environment where students feel safe to take risks, make mistakes, and ask questions. Encourage an atmosphere of mutual respect, kindness, and inclusivity. This environment promotes self-expression and builds students' confidence.

5. Provide Opportunities for Success: Offer a range of activities and tasks that allow students to experience success. Differentiate instruction to meet individual needs and provide opportunities for students to excel in areas where they have strengths and interests.

6. Cultivate Positive Relationships: Build positive relationships with students based on trust, respect, and care. Get to know them individually, show genuine interest in their well-being, and create a supportive teacher-student connection. These relationships foster a sense of belonging and boost confidence.

7. Encourage Self-Reflection and Self-Evaluation: Guide students in reflecting on their own progress and achievements. Encourage them to evaluate their strengths, identify areas for improvement, and set personal goals. This self-awareness helps students build confidence in their abilities and take ownership of their learning.

8. Promote Peer Collaboration and Support: Encourage students to collaborate and support one another. Foster a classroom culture where students celebrate each other's successes and provide constructive feedback. Peer support and recognition contribute to building students' confidence.

9. Scaffold Learning: Provide appropriate support and scaffolding to help students gradually build skills and confidence. Offer guided practice, modelling, and feedback

as students work through new concepts or tasks. Gradually release responsibility to foster independent learning and confidence.

10.   Teach Growth Mind-set: Promote a growth mind-set by teaching students that abilities can be developed through effort and practice. Encourage them to embrace challenges, view mistakes as learning opportunities, and believe in their capacity to improve.

11.   Encourage Public Speaking and Presentations: Provide opportunities for students to engage in public speaking or presentations. Start with low-pressure activities and gradually increase the level of challenge. Provide guidance, practice, and constructive feedback to help students build confidence in their communication skills.

12.   Celebrate Effort and Achievements: Celebrate students' efforts and achievements publicly. Recognise their progress, growth, and contributions in front of their peers and the school community. Public recognition boosts confidence and motivates further success.

By employing these techniques and skills, educators can create a positive and empowering learning environment where students' confidence flourishes. Building students' confidence not only supports their academic performance but also nurtures their overall self-esteem and resilience

Establishing a safe and inclusive environment for students

Establishing a safe and inclusive environment is essential for promoting positive learning experiences and the overall well-being of students. Here are some ways a teacher can go about creating a safe and inclusive environment:

Set Clear Expectations: Communicate clear expectations for behaviour and interactions in the classroom. Establish ground rules that promote respect, kindness, and inclusivity. Make sure students understand and actively participate in creating a safe and inclusive classroom culture.

Foster Positive Relationships: Build positive relationships with students based on trust, respect, and empathy. Get to know students individually, show genuine interest in their lives and experiences, and actively listen to their concerns and perspectives.

Establish Norms for Respectful Communication: Teach and model respectful communication skills. Encourage students to listen attentively, take turns speaking, and express their ideas and opinions respectfully. Address any instances of bullying, harassment, or disrespectful behaviour promptly and consistently.

Create an Inclusive Curriculum: Design and deliver a curriculum that reflects the diversity of your students. Include diverse perspectives, cultures, and experiences in your teaching materials and instructional approaches. Ensure that all students can see themselves represented and valued in the classroom.

Encourage Student Voice and Agency: Provide opportunities for students to express their thoughts, ideas, and concerns. Foster a sense of ownership in their learning by involving them in decision-making processes, such as selecting topics or projects. Actively seek and incorporate their input and feedback.

Promote Collaboration and Cooperation: Foster a collaborative learning environment where students work together, respect one another's ideas, and support each other's learning. Provide opportunities for group work, discussions, and cooperative learning activities that promote teamwork and inclusivity.

Address Bias and Stereotypes: Be aware of your own biases and actively work to counter stereotypes or discriminatory attitudes in the classroom. Challenge biases and promote inclusivity by providing counter-narratives, promoting understanding, and encouraging critical thinking about stereotypes.

Create Physical and Emotional Safety: Ensure that the physical environment is safe, comfortable, and conducive to learning. Establish clear procedures for handling emergencies, and enforce rules to prevent physical or emotional harm. Foster a sense of emotional safety by encouraging open communication, empathy, and understanding.

Incorporate Multicultural Perspectives: Integrate multicultural perspectives and resources into your teaching. Incorporate diverse literature, music, art, and historical narratives from different cultures and backgrounds. Encourage students to share their cultural experiences and celebrate diversity.

Provide Support for Individual Needs: Recognise and support the individual needs of all students. Differentiate instruction to accommodate diverse learning styles, abilities, and interests. Provide additional support or accommodations as needed for students with disabilities or unique learning requirements.

Offer Professional Development: Engage in ongoing professional development to enhance your own cultural competence, awareness, and knowledge. Stay updated on best practices for creating safe and inclusive environments and advocate for inclusive education within your school community.

Build Community Partnerships: Collaborate with families, community Organisations, and other professionals to foster a safe and inclusive environment beyond the classroom. Engage in partnerships that promote cultural understanding, address equity issues, and provide resources and support for all students.

By implementing these strategies, educators can create a safe and inclusive environment where students feel respected, valued, and empowered to learn and grow. This fosters a positive classroom climate and enhances students' overall well-being and academic success.

Teaching students how to use technology effectively is crucial in today's digital age. Here are some strategies to help teach students how to use technology effectively:

Set Clear Expectations: Clearly communicate expectations for technology use, including appropriate behaviour, responsible use, and adherence to school policies or guidelines. Establish guidelines for internet safety, digital citizenship, and online etiquette.

Provide Digital Literacy Instruction: Teach students fundamental digital literacy skills, such as navigating digital interfaces, using search engines effectively, evaluating online information for credibility, and practicing good cyber hygiene (e.g., password security, avoiding phishing attempts).

Model Effective Technology Use: Model proper use of technology by demonstrating how to use various tools, software, or platforms. Show students how to find, analyse, and use digital resources responsibly. Demonstrate effective strategies for problem-solving and troubleshooting.

Integrate Technology Across the Curriculum: Integrate technology seamlessly into instructional activities across subject areas. Show students how technology can enhance their learning, creativity, collaboration, and critical thinking skills. Design lessons that incorporate technology as a tool for research, multimedia creation, data analysis, or communication.

Teach Digital Organisation and Productivity: Guide students in using technology to stay Organised and manage their workload effectively. Teach them strategies for digital note-taking, file Organisation, time management tools, and online collaboration platforms. Help students leverage technology to streamline their academic tasks.

Foster Digital Collaboration: Promote collaboration and communication among students using technology tools. Teach them how to work collaboratively on shared documents, use online discussion boards or forums, and participate in virtual group projects. Emphasise the importance of respectful and effective online communication.

Develop Media Literacy Skills: Help students develop critical thinking skills to evaluate and analyse media messages. Teach them how to identify bias, recognise persuasive techniques, and distinguish between reliable and unreliable sources. Encourage students to be discerning consumers of digital media.

Encourage Creativity and Innovation: Empower students to use technology as a creative tool. Provide opportunities for them to create multimedia projects, design digital presentations, code interactive programs, or develop digital art. Encourage exploration and experimentation with various technology tools and platforms.

Foster Responsible Digital Citizenship: Teach students about their rights, responsibilities, and ethical behaviour in the digital world. Promote digital citizenship skills such as respecting privacy, practicing online safety, addressing cyberbullying, and being responsible digital community members.

Provide Ongoing Support and Professional Development: Offer ongoing support and resources for students to enhance their technology skills. Provide tutorials, workshops, or online resources for students to develop specific technology competencies. Stay updated with current technology trends and seek professional development opportunities to enhance your own skills as an educator.

Encourage Reflective Practice: Promote reflection on technology use and its impact on learning. Encourage students to reflect on their digital experiences, evaluate the effectiveness of the tools they use, and consider the ethical implications of technology in society. Help them become critical and responsible users of technology.

Emphasise Digital Well-being: Discuss the importance of maintaining a healthy balance in technology use. Teach students strategies for managing screen time, practicing digital self-care, and fostering healthy relationships both online and offline. Encourage them to be mindful of their digital footprint and practice digital well-being.

By implementing these strategies, you can empower students to become responsible, critical, and effective users of technology. This equips them with the skills and mind-set necessary to navigate the digital world and leverage technology for their personal growth and academic success

Incorporating multimedia resources in the teaching plan

Incorporating multimedia resources in teaching can enhance engagement, comprehension, and retention of information. Here's how educators can incorporate multimedia resources in their teaching plans:

1. Determine Learning Objectives: Identify the specific learning objectives or concepts you want to address in your lesson. This will guide your selection of multimedia resources that align with the content and skills you intend to teach.

2. Choose Appropriate Multimedia Formats: Consider the different multimedia formats that can support your lesson, such as videos, images, audio clips, animations, infographics, simulations, or interactive websites. Select formats that best convey the content and engage students.

3. Select High-Quality Resources: Use reputable sources and high-quality multimedia resources that are accurate, relevant, and age-appropriate. Ensure the resources align with your teaching goals and provide clear, concise, and reliable information.

4. Integrate Multimedia into Lesson Sequences: Determine where and how you will integrate multimedia resources within your lesson plan. Consider whether you will use them as an introduction, during instruction, for reinforcement, or as a conclusion. Ensure a logical flow and purposeful integration of multimedia throughout the lesson.

5. Provide Context and Pre-Viewing Guidance: Before showing or using a multimedia resource, provide context and purpose for its use. Preview the resource with students, guiding their attention to specific elements or questions they should consider while engaging with the multimedia content.

6. Engage Students Actively: Encourage active engagement with multimedia resources. Incorporate reflection prompts, discussion questions, or interactive elements that require students to interact with the content, apply critical thinking skills, and make connections to their prior knowledge.

7. Scaffold Understanding: Support students in making meaning from the multimedia resources by scaffolding their understanding. Pause the multimedia resource at strategic points to clarify concepts, ask comprehension questions, or facilitate discussions. Provide additional explanations or examples as needed.

8. Encourage Note-Taking or Annotation: Encourage students to take notes or annotate while engaging with multimedia resources. This helps them process information, highlight key points, and make connections to the content being presented.

9. Facilitate Discussion and Reflection: After engaging with the multimedia resource, facilitate class discussions or reflective activities to deepen students' understanding and

help them make connections to the broader learning goals. Encourage students to share their thoughts, ask questions, and relate the multimedia content to real-life examples or personal experiences.

10. Provide Opportunities for Student Creation: Encourage students to create their own multimedia resources as part of the learning process. This can include creating videos, podcasts, digital presentations, or interactive graphics to demonstrate their understanding of the content.

11. Assess Learning with Multimedia: Incorporate assessments that utilise multimedia formats to evaluate student learning. This can include tasks such as creating multimedia presentations, analysing multimedia resources for accuracy or bias, or producing multimedia projects that demonstrate mastery of the content.

12. Reflect and Revise: Reflect on the effectiveness of the multimedia resources used in your teaching. Gather student feedback, monitor their engagement and comprehension, and make adjustments to your teaching plan accordingly. Continuously seek new and innovative multimedia resources to enhance your teaching practice.

By incorporating multimedia resources into teaching plans, educators can leverage the power of visuals, audio, and interactive elements to engage students, promote deeper understanding, and facilitate meaningful learning experiences.

What actions, techniques do educators use in class for Active participation strategies?

Educators use various actions and techniques in the classroom to encourage active participation from students. Here are some effective strategies:

Think-Pair-Share: Pose a question or problem to students and give them a few moments to think individually. Then, have them discuss their thoughts with a partner before sharing their ideas with the whole class. This strategy promotes active engagement, collaboration, and the opportunity for all students to participate.

Classroom Discussions: Facilitate whole-class discussions by encouraging students to express their thoughts, opinions, and questions. Use open-ended questions, follow-up prompts, and active listening techniques to encourage student contributions and create a safe environment for sharing ideas.

Questioning Techniques: Use a variety of questioning techniques to stimulate active participation. Ask higher-order thinking questions that require students to analyse, evaluate, and apply knowledge. Encourage students to provide reasoning and evidence to support their answers.

Cooperative Learning: Incorporate cooperative learning activities where students work in groups to solve problems, complete projects, or discuss concepts. Assign roles within the group to ensure everyone has a task and encourage equal participation from all members.

Hands-On Activities: Engage students in hands-on activities that require active involvement and manipulation of materials. This can include experiments, simulations, role-plays, or interactive games. Hands-on activities promote engagement, exploration, and critical thinking.

Response Cards or Whiteboards: Provide students with individual response cards or whiteboards to write and display their answers or ideas. This allows all students to participate simultaneously and encourages active thinking and sharing of responses.

Brainstorming Sessions: Conduct brainstorming sessions where students generate a list of ideas, solutions, or possibilities related to a topic. Create a non-judgmental environment where all ideas are accepted, fostering creativity, and active participation.

Jigsaw Technique: Divide students into small groups, assign each group a specific topic or concept, and have them become experts in that area. Then, reassemble the groups, ensuring that each group has a representative from each topic. Students share their expertise, promoting collaboration and active participation.

Gallery Walks: Create stations or displays around the classroom with different materials or prompts related to the topic. Have students rotate through the stations in small groups, actively engaging with the materials, and discussing their findings or observations.

Simulations or Role-Plays: Engage students in simulations or role-plays where they take on different roles or perspectives related to the topic being studied. This strategy encourages active participation, critical thinking, and empathy.

Use Technology Tools: Incorporate technology tools and platforms that promote active participation, such as online discussion forums, interactive polling or response systems, collaborative document sharing, or multimedia creation tools. These tools can increase student engagement and provide opportunities for active involvement.

Peer Teaching and Presentations: Assign students the task of teaching a concept or presenting their understanding of a topic to their peers. This not only encourages active participation from the presenters but also engages the audience through listening, questioning, and discussion.

By implementing these strategies, educators can create a classroom environment that encourages active participation from all students. Active participation fosters deeper understanding, critical thinking, and a sense of ownership over the learning process. It also promotes collaboration, communication, and the development of important social and cognitive skills

Scaffolding Instruction

Scaffolding instruction is a teaching strategy that involves providing temporary support and guidance to students as they learn new concepts or skills. The goal is to help students build their understanding and competence, gradually reducing the support as they become more independent learners. Scaffolding instruction aims to bridge the gap between what students already know and what they need to learn.

Here are key components and techniques involved in scaffolding instruction:

Assess Prior Knowledge: Before introducing new content, assess students' prior knowledge and understanding related to the topic. This helps determine the appropriate starting point for instruction and identifies any misconceptions that may need to be addressed.

Chunking and Sequencing: Break down complex concepts or skills into smaller, manageable chunks. Present information in a logical sequence, building upon previous knowledge and skills. Each chunk should be scaffolded before moving on to the next, ensuring students grasp one concept before moving to the next.

Provide Clear Instructions and Models: Clearly explain the learning objectives and provide step-by-step instructions. Use models, examples, and demonstrations to illustrate concepts or processes. Show students what the final outcome should look like or how the task should be performed.

Offer Guided Practice: Engage students in guided practice activities that allow them to apply new knowledge and skills with support. Provide prompts, cues, or templates to help them structure their thinking or work. Offer feedback and correction as needed to guide their progress.

Use Prompts and Questioning: Pose thought-provoking questions or prompts to stimulate critical thinking and guide students' exploration. Ask questions that encourage students to make connections, analyse information, or apply concepts. This prompts deeper understanding and helps students develop higher-order thinking skills.

Provide Graphic Organisers or Visual Aids: Use graphic Organisers, visual aids, or concept maps to help students Organise and represent their thinking. These tools provide a visual structure that supports comprehension and helps students make connections between ideas.

Offer Scaffolding Tools and Resources: Provide additional resources, such as reference materials, graphic Organisers, or vocabulary lists, to support students' understanding and independent learning. These tools act as support structures that students can rely on as they develop their skills.

Foster Collaboration: Encourage peer collaboration and discussion during scaffolded activities. Group students with different levels of proficiency, allowing more experienced students to assist and scaffold their peers. Collaboration provides opportunities for students to learn from one another and strengthen their understanding.

Gradually Release Responsibility: As students become more proficient, gradually reduce the level of support and increase their autonomy. Transition from guided practice to independent practice, allowing students to apply their learning without constant scaffolding. Monitor their progress and provide support as needed.

Monitor and Adjust Instruction: Continuously assess students' progress and understanding. Adjust instruction and scaffolding techniques based on their needs. Provide additional support or challenge as required, adapting to individual learning styles and preferences.
Scaffolding instruction is a dynamic process that adapts to the needs of individual students.

It supports their development by providing just enough support to foster learning and independence. As students gain confidence and competence, they gradually assume more responsibility for their learning, eventually becoming independent learners in the targeted area.

Individualising Instruction

A teacher may individualise instruction to meet the unique needs, abilities, learning styles, and interests of each student. Here are some reasons why a teacher might choose to individualise instruction:

Addressing Diverse Learning Needs: Students come with diverse backgrounds, abilities, and learning profiles. Individualising instruction allows educators to tailor their teaching methods and materials to accommodate the specific needs of each student. This ensures that all students have the opportunity to learn and progress at their own pace.

Promoting Student Engagement and Motivation: Individualised instruction can increase student engagement and motivation. When students feel that their learning is personalised and relevant to their interests and strengths, they are more likely to be actively involved in the learning process and feel a sense of ownership over their education.

Fostering a Positive Learning Environment: Individualising instruction can create a positive learning environment where students feel supported, valued, and understood. By considering students' individual needs, educators can build rapport, enhance self-esteem, and promote a culture of respect and inclusivity.

Differentiating Instruction: Individualising instruction enables educators to differentiate their approach to teaching, ensuring that all students are appropriately challenged and supported. By adjusting content, tasks, and instructional strategies, educators can meet students where they are academically and provide opportunities for growth and success.

Catering to Learning Styles and Preferences: Students have different learning styles and preferences. Individualising instruction allows educators to present information and provide learning experiences that align with students' preferred modes of learning, whether visual, auditory, kinaesthetic, or a combination thereof.

Accommodating Special Needs: Some students may have specific learning disabilities, exceptionalities, or special needs. Individualising instruction helps educators provide accommodations, modifications, or specialised supports to ensure that these students can access the curriculum and achieve their learning goals.

Encouraging Self-Regulated Learning: Individualised instruction fosters self-regulated learning skills in students. By providing opportunities for students to make choices, set goals, and monitor their progress, educators help students develop important skills such as self-reflection, time management, and self-advocacy.

Enhancing Academic Performance: By addressing individual needs and providing targeted instruction, educators can optimise student learning outcomes. Individualising instruction can lead to improved academic performance, as students receive the support and challenges they need to thrive.

Nurturing Talent and Giftedness: Individualising instruction allows educators to identify and nurture the talents and gifts of high-achieving or gifted students. By providing extension activities, enrichment opportunities, or specialised projects, educators can cater to these students' unique abilities and foster their intellectual growth.

Developing a Lifelong Love of Learning: Individualised instruction can help cultivate a lifelong love of learning. By tailoring instruction to students' interests, strengths, and aspirations, educators can create an environment that promotes curiosity, exploration, and a desire for continuous learning.

Individualising instruction recognises the diverse needs and abilities of students and ensures that each student has the opportunity to reach their full potential. It supports student success, engagement, and well-being by valuing and honouring the individuality of each learner.

To encourage student autonomy, educators can employ various strategies that promote independence, self-directed learning, and decision-making. Here's how educators can foster student autonomy:

1. Gradually Release Responsibility: Gradually transition from teacher-led instruction to student-led learning by releasing responsibility to students. Start with explicit instruction and gradually shift towards guided practice and independent application of knowledge and skills.

2. Set Clear Expectations: Clearly communicate expectations for student autonomy, including the level of independence expected and the criteria for success. Help students understand that they are responsible for their learning and decision-making, within the boundaries set by the teacher.

3. Foster a Supportive Environment: Create a supportive classroom environment where students feel safe to take risks, make mistakes, and learn from them. Encourage open communication, collaboration, and respect for diverse ideas and perspectives.

4. Promote Goal Setting: Teach students how to set goals that are specific, measurable, achievable, relevant, and time-bound (SMART goals). Encourage them to set both short-term and long-term goals related to their academic progress, personal growth, and areas of interest.

5. Develop Self-Regulation Skills: Help students develop self-regulation skills, such as self-monitoring, self-reflection, and self-assessment. Teach them strategies for managing their time, Organising their tasks, and staying focused on their goals.

6. Provide Choices and Options: Offer students choices within the learning process whenever possible. Provide options for assignments, projects, or research topics that align with their interests and strengths. This promotes a sense of ownership and autonomy in their learning.

7. Encourage Critical Thinking: Promote critical thinking and problem-solving skills by posing open-ended questions, challenging assumptions, and encouraging students to analyse, evaluate, and synthesize information. Help them develop the ability to think independently and make informed decisions.

8. Foster Self-Directed Learning: Provide opportunities for self-directed learning experiences, such as inquiry-based projects or independent research. Support students in identifying their learning needs, locating resources, and managing their learning process.

9.   Facilitate Peer Collaboration: Encourage collaborative learning activities where students work together, share ideas, and learn from one another. Foster a classroom culture that values peer feedback, discussion, and cooperation. Collaboration provides opportunities for students to develop autonomy while learning from their peers.

10.   Offer Guidance and Support: Act as a guide and facilitator, rather than a dispenser of knowledge. Provide guidance and support when students encounter challenges or need clarification. Encourage them to seek help, explore resources independently, and take ownership of their learning.

11.   Reflect and Self-Evaluate: Encourage students to reflect on their learning experiences, assess their progress, and identify areas for growth. Teach them how to self-evaluate their work, provide constructive feedback to themselves, and set new learning goals based on their reflections.

12.   Celebrate Autonomy and Growth: Recognise and celebrate students' autonomy and growth in their learning journey. Acknowledge their efforts, progress, and accomplishments, fostering a sense of pride, confidence, and intrinsic motivation.

By implementing these strategies, educators empower students to take ownership of their learning, make informed decisions, and become self-directed learners. Developing student autonomy not only supports academic success but also cultivates skills and qualities that contribute to lifelong learning and personal growth

Effective classroom management involves a combination of skills and techniques to create a positive and productive learning environment. Here are some essential skills and techniques that educators use for classroom management:

1. Establish Clear Expectations: Set clear and consistent expectations for behaviour and academic performance from the beginning of the school year. Communicate these expectations to students and ensure they understand the rules and consequences for both positive and negative behaviours.

2. Build Positive Relationships: Develop positive relationships with students based on trust, respect, and care. Get to know your students as individuals, show interest in their lives, and listen to their concerns and ideas. A positive teacher-student relationship fosters a supportive classroom atmosphere.

3. Use Positive Reinforcement: Recognise and reinforce positive behaviours through praise, rewards, and encouragement. Positive reinforcement motivates students to engage in desired behaviours and creates a positive classroom climate.

4. Classroom Routines and Procedures: Establish clear and consistent routines and procedures for everyday tasks, such as entering the classroom, transitioning between activities, and packing up at the end of the day. Clearly explain these routines to students and practice them until they become familiar.

5. Proximity and Body Language: Use proximity to manage behaviour. Being physically present near students who may need additional support or redirection can prevent potential disruptions. Positive body language, such as eye contact and open gestures, communicates approachability and attentiveness.

6. Use Verbal and Non-Verbal Cues: Develop a repertoire of verbal and non-verbal cues to manage behaviour. For example, using a specific hand signal or raising your voice slightly to get students' attention. Non-verbal cues can be less intrusive than speaking aloud and help maintain the flow of instruction.

7. Encourage Active Engagement: Plan engaging lessons that keep students interested and involved in their learning. Incorporate hands-on activities, group work, discussions, multimedia resources, and interactive learning experiences to promote active engagement.

8. Differentiate Instruction: Differentiate instruction to meet the diverse needs of students in the classroom. Provide activities and materials that cater to various learning styles, abilities, and interests. Individualising instruction helps keep all students engaged and motivated.

9.   Address Misbehaviour Proactively: When dealing with misbehaviour, address it proactively and respectfully. Use restorative practices and encourage students to take responsibility for their actions. Focus on finding solutions and helping students learn from their mistakes.

10.   Time Management: Efficiently manage time during lessons to keep students engaged and on track. Have a clear plan for each lesson, with time allocations for different activities. Be flexible to adjust the pace if needed to maintain student engagement.

11.   Encourage Student Voice: Give students opportunities to express their opinions, ask questions, and share their ideas. Encouraging student voice and choice in the classroom empowers them and fosters a sense of ownership over their learning.

12.   Continuously reflect and improve: Regularly reflect on your classroom management strategies and adjust them based on the needs of your students. Seek feedback from colleagues, students, and parents to continually improve your approach.

Effective classroom management creates an environment where students feel supported, respected, and motivated to learn. By utilising these skills and techniques, educators can establish a positive and productive classroom climate that maximises student learning and growth.

Conflict in a teaching environment

In a teaching environment, various types of conflicts may arise among students, between students and educators, or among educators themselves. Here are some common types of conflicts that can occur:

Interpersonal Conflicts: These conflicts arise between individuals and can stem from differences in personalities, values, communication styles, or personal preferences. Interpersonal conflicts may involve disagreements, misunderstandings, or clashes of interests between students or between students and educators.

Academic or Task-related Conflicts: Conflicts related to academic tasks can arise when students have different ideas or approaches to completing assignments, projects, or group work. Differences in work styles, expectations, or contributions can lead to conflicts related to academic tasks or responsibilities.

Power Struggles: Power struggles can occur when there is a perceived imbalance of power or authority. This can manifest as conflicts between students vying for leadership roles or conflicts between students and educators over classroom rules, discipline, or decision-making.

Bullying or Harassment: Instances of bullying or harassment, such as verbal or physical aggression, exclusion, or discriminatory behaviour, can occur in the teaching environment. These conflicts may require immediate intervention to ensure the safety and well-being of all students involved.

Classroom Management Conflicts: Conflicts may arise due to differences in expectations, rules, or classroom procedures. Students may challenge or resist classroom management strategies, leading to conflicts with educators or among students.

Cultural or Diversity Conflicts: Conflicts can arise when there are cultural, ethnic, or religious differences among students or between students and educators. Misunderstandings, stereotypes, or lack of cultural awareness can contribute to these conflicts.

Communication Breakdowns: Communication breakdowns can lead to conflicts when there are misunderstandings, misinterpretations, or ineffective communication between individuals. Differences in communication styles, language barriers, or ineffective listening can contribute to these conflicts.

Professional Disputes: Conflicts among educators or between educators and administrators may occur over issues such as curriculum decisions, teaching methodologies, grading policies, or resource allocation. These conflicts can impact the overall functioning of the educational institution.

Parent-Teacher Conflicts: Conflicts may arise between educators and parents when there are differing expectations, concerns about student performance, or disagreements regarding classroom policies or disciplinary actions.

Organisational Conflicts: Conflicts related to Organisational structures, policies, or administrative decisions can occur within the educational institution. These conflicts may involve disagreements over budgeting, resource allocation, scheduling, or changes in curriculum or assessment practices.

It is important for educators to be aware of these potential conflicts and have strategies in place to address and resolve them effectively. Creating a positive and inclusive classroom climate, promoting open communication, and teaching conflict resolution skills can help prevent and manage conflicts in the teaching environment.

Conflict resolution skills are crucial for educators to address and resolve conflicts that may arise in the classroom. Here are some skills and techniques that educators can use for effective conflict resolution:

Active Listening: Actively listen to all parties involved in the conflict without interruption. Provide opportunities for each person to express their perspective, feelings, and concerns. Show empathy and understanding to foster a cooperative atmosphere.

Neutral and Non-Judgmental Approach: Maintain a neutral and non-judgmental stance when addressing conflicts. Avoid taking sides or assigning blame. Focus on understanding the underlying issues and finding a resolution that benefits all parties involved.

Problem-Solving and Mediation: Guide students through the problem-solving process, encouraging them to identify the root causes of the conflict and generate potential solutions. Act as a mediator, facilitating the negotiation and helping students find a mutually acceptable resolution.

Establish Ground Rules: Set clear ground rules for conflict resolution discussions. Establish guidelines for respectful communication, active listening, and taking turns to speak. Ensure that all parties have an equal opportunity to contribute to the resolution process.

Empathy and Perspective-Taking: Encourage students to empathise with each other by considering the other person's perspective and feelings. Help them see the conflict from multiple viewpoints to foster understanding and empathy.

Effective Communication: Teach and model effective communication skills, such as using "I" statements to express feelings and needs, active listening, and assertive but respectful communication. Guide students in expressing their thoughts and concerns constructively, without resorting to personal attacks.

Collaborative Problem-Solving: Encourage students to work collaboratively to find solutions rather than imposing a resolution. Guide them in brainstorming ideas, evaluating options, and reaching a consensus. Emphasise the importance of compromise and seeking win-win outcomes.

Time and Space for Reflection: Allow time and space for reflection before and during conflict resolution discussions. This gives students an opportunity to calm down, gather their thoughts, and approach the situation with a clearer perspective.

Restorative Justice Practices: Incorporate restorative justice practices to promote accountability, understanding, and healing. Focus on repairing relationships and addressing the harm caused by the conflict. Encourage students to take responsibility for their actions and explore ways to make amends.

Follow-Up and Support: Follow up with students after conflict resolution to ensure that the agreed-upon solutions are implemented and the conflict does not resurface. Provide ongoing support and guidance to help students develop effective conflict resolution skills.

Teach Conflict Resolution Skills: Integrate conflict resolution skills into the curriculum or dedicated lessons. Teach students about effective communication, problem-solving, empathy, and negotiation skills. Provide opportunities for role-playing or simulations to practice these skills in a controlled environment.

Encourage Respectful Classroom Culture: Create a classroom culture that values respect, empathy, and open communication from the beginning of the school year. Foster a sense of community, where differences are celebrated, and conflicts are seen as opportunities for growth and learning.

By utilising these skills and techniques, educators can effectively address and resolve conflicts in the classroom. By teaching students how to navigate conflicts constructively, educators empower them with lifelong skills that promote healthy relationships, empathy, and effective communication

Collaborative learning techniques involve students working together in groups or pairs to achieve a common learning goal. These techniques promote active engagement, critical thinking, communication, and teamwork skills. Here are some collaborative learning techniques and examples of how they can be used:

1. Think-Pair-Share: Students individually reflect on a question or prompt, and then pair up to discuss their thoughts with a partner. Finally, pairs share their ideas with the whole class. This technique encourages active participation, peer interaction, and the opportunity for students to learn from each other.

2. Jigsaw: Divide students into small groups, each responsible for mastering a specific subtopic. After becoming experts in their assigned subtopic, students regroup with peers who studied different subtopics. Each student then teaches their new group about their assigned subtopic. This promotes collaboration, research skills, and a comprehensive understanding of the topic.

3. Group Projects: Assign students to work together in groups to complete a project or solve a problem. The project should require collaboration, division of tasks, and collective decision-making. This technique fosters teamwork, communication, and problem-solving skills.

4. Peer Teaching: Have students take turns teaching a concept or skill to their peers. This can involve preparing a mini-lesson, delivering a presentation, or creating a tutorial. Peer teaching enhances understanding, promotes active engagement, and helps students develop communication and leadership skills.

5. Collaborative Writing: Divide students into pairs or small groups to collectively write a story, essay, or research paper. Each student contributes to the writing process, discussing ideas, editing, and revising together. Collaborative writing encourages critical thinking, negotiation, and shared responsibility for the final product.

6. Roundtable Discussions: Students sit in a circle and engage in a facilitated discussion on a specific topic. Each student has an opportunity to share their thoughts or respond to prompts while others actively listen. This technique promotes respectful dialogue, critical thinking, and the exploration of different perspectives.

7. Problem-Based Learning: Present students with a real-world problem or scenario that requires collaborative problem-solving. Students work together to analyse the problem, propose solutions, and present their findings. This technique enhances critical thinking, teamwork, and application of knowledge.

8. Peer Editing: Students exchange their written work with a partner and provide feedback on each other's drafts. They offer suggestions for improvement, check for errors, and

help each other refine their work. Peer editing develops editing skills, encourages constructive feedback, and promotes a sense of shared responsibility for quality work.

9.   Learning Stations: Create learning stations with different activities or tasks related to the topic. Divide students into small groups and assign them to rotate through the stations. Each group engages in a different activity and collaborates to complete tasks or solve problems. Learning stations encourage active participation, exploration, and collaboration.

10.   Simulations or Role-Plays: Students engage in simulations or role-plays where they assume different roles or perspectives related to a topic. This technique promotes collaboration, critical thinking, and empathy as students work together to solve problems or negotiate different viewpoints.

When using collaborative learning techniques, it is important to set clear expectations, establish group norms, provide guidance, and monitor group dynamics to ensure productive collaboration. Educators can facilitate discussions, provide structure, offer support, and assess individual and group learning outcomes to maximise the benefits of collaborative learning

Questioning techniques when teaching?

Educators use a variety of questioning techniques to engage students, stimulate critical thinking, promote deeper understanding, and assess learning. Here are some common questioning techniques used in teaching:

1. Open-Ended Questions: Pose questions that require more than a simple "yes" or "no" answer. Open-ended questions encourage students to think critically, express their thoughts, provide explanations, or explore multiple perspectives. For example, "Why do you think the character made that decision?" or "What evidence can you find to support your argument?"

2. Probing Questions: Use probing questions to delve deeper into students' thinking or to elicit more specific information. Probing questions encourage students to provide more details, evidence, or reasoning to support their answers. Examples include: "Can you explain your reasoning further?" or "What led you to that conclusion?"

3. Socratic Questions: Inspired by the Socratic Method, these questions prompt students to analyse and evaluate ideas, assumptions, and evidence. Socratic questions challenge students' thinking and help them develop critical thinking skills. Examples include: "What are the strengths and weaknesses of that argument?" or "How does this relate to what we've learned before?"

4. Reflective Questions: Encourage students to reflect on their learning experiences and make connections to their prior knowledge. Reflective questions promote metacognition and help students monitor their understanding and learning progress. Examples include: "What was the most challenging part of this task, and how did you overcome it?" or "How does this new concept relate to what you already know?"

5. Hypothetical Questions: Pose hypothetical scenarios or "what if" questions to stimulate creative thinking, problem-solving, and the exploration of possibilities. Hypothetical questions encourage students to apply their knowledge in new contexts and think critically about potential outcomes. For example, "What might have happened if historical event X had occurred differently?"

6. Clarifying Questions: Use clarifying questions to ensure students understand the information or instructions given. These questions help identify any areas of confusion or misconceptions and allow educators to provide further explanations or examples. Examples include: "Can you rephrase that in your own words?" or "What specific part of the problem is unclear to you?"

7. Predictive Questions: Encourage students to make predictions or hypotheses based on their knowledge and understanding. Predictive questions help students develop their analytical skills and logical reasoning. For example, "What do you think will happen next in the story? Why do you think so?"

8. Higher-Order Thinking Questions: Pose questions that require students to engage in critical thinking, analysis, synthesis, and evaluation. Higher-order thinking questions challenge students to go beyond simple recall and encourage deeper understanding and application of knowledge. Examples include: "How would you justify your solution using evidence from multiple sources?" or "What alternative perspectives could be considered?"

9. Guiding Questions: Provide guiding questions that help students navigate complex tasks or problem-solving activities. These questions provide a framework or structure for thinking, Organising ideas, or approaching a task. For example, "What steps could you take to solve this problem?" or "What factors should you consider when making a decision?"

10. Extension Questions: Pose questions that extend students' thinking beyond the basic concepts and encourage them to make connections, draw conclusions, or apply knowledge in new contexts. Extension questions promote higher-level thinking and critical analysis. Examples include: "How does this concept apply to real-life situations?" or "What are the implications of this discovery?"

When using questioning techniques, it is important to give students enough wait time to process and respond. Encourage all students to participate, use a mix of teacher-guided and student-generated questions, and provide feedback or follow-up questions to deepen understanding. Effective questioning stimulates student engagement, promotes critical thinking, and fosters meaningful classroom discussions.

Visual aids and Props in the classroom

Educators can use a variety of visual aids and props in the classroom to enhance learning, engage students, and make abstract concepts more concrete. Here are some examples:

1. Whiteboard or Blackboard: These traditional visual aids are versatile and can be used to write and illustrate key points, diagrams, or equations during a lesson. They allow for real-time interaction and discussion.

2. Projector and Screen: Educators can use a projector and screen to display slideshows, videos, interactive websites, or educational software to support their lessons. This technology enables the sharing of visual content with the whole class.

3. Posters and Charts: Displaying posters and charts on classroom walls can provide visual references for students. They can include maps, timelines, vocabulary words, grammar rules, or scientific diagrams to support learning and serve as visual reminders.

4. Models and Manipulatives: Three-dimensional models or manipulatives help students understand abstract concepts by providing a tactile and visual representation. For example, using fraction bars or cubes for math, or a globe to explore geography.

5. Graphs and Charts: Presenting information in the form of graphs, charts, or infographics can help students interpret and analyse data. These visual aids can be used to illustrate trends, compare data, or support scientific findings.

6. Visual Timelines: Timelines visually represent the sequence of events, historical periods, or a chronological order of topics. They help students grasp the progression and relationships between different events or concepts.

7. Maps and Globes: Maps and globes are essential for geography lessons. They allow students to visualise and explore different countries, continents, or physical features of the world. Interactive maps on digital devices can also be used.

8. Real-Life Objects and Artefacts: Bringing in real-life objects or artefacts related to a lesson topic can create a tangible connection to the content. For example, bringing in fossils for a lesson on dinosaurs or historical artefacts for a history lesson.

9. Visual Presentations and Slides: Creating visually appealing slides or presentations using software tools like PowerPoint or Google Slides can enhance student engagement and understanding. Incorporate images, graphics, diagrams, and text to support key points.

10. Flashcards: Flashcards are handy visual aids for vocabulary building, language learning, or memorising key concepts. They can include images, words, definitions, or example sentences.

11.   Videos and Multimedia: Utilise educational videos, animations, or multimedia resources to support and reinforce learning. These visual aids can bring complex concepts to life and cater to different learning styles.

12.   Digital Interactive Tools: Online interactive tools, simulations, or virtual reality experiences can provide immersive visual experiences and enhance understanding in subjects such as science, history, or art.

When using visual aids and props, it is important to ensure they are relevant, well-Organised, and visually appealing. Introduce them at the appropriate times during the lesson to support specific learning objectives. Incorporating a variety of visual aids and props helps accommodate different learning styles, reinforce concepts, and create an engaging and interactive learning environment

Creating a positive classroom culture is essential for fostering a supportive, inclusive, and engaging learning environment. Here are some strategies that educators can use to cultivate a positive classroom culture:

1. Establish Clear Expectations: Clearly communicate and collaboratively establish classroom expectations and rules at the beginning of the school year. Involve students in the process to promote ownership and understanding. Reinforce these expectations consistently throughout the year.

2. Model Positive Behaviour: Be a positive role model for students by demonstrating respect, kindness, empathy, and fairness in your interactions with students and colleagues. Model effective communication, active listening, and problem-solving skills.

3. Build Relationships: Develop positive relationships with your students by getting to know them individually. Show genuine interest in their lives, cultures, interests, and backgrounds. Regularly check in with students and provide opportunities for one-on-one interactions.

4. Encourage Student Voice and Choice: Create opportunities for students to share their thoughts, ideas, and opinions. Value their contributions and encourage active participation in class discussions, decision-making, and problem-solving. Incorporate student choice and autonomy whenever possible.

5. Promote Inclusivity and Respect: Foster an inclusive classroom environment where every student feels valued, respected, and safe. Celebrate diversity, teach and model acceptance, and address any instances of discrimination or bullying promptly and appropriately.

6. Establish Collaborative Learning Opportunities: Encourage collaborative learning activities that promote teamwork, cooperation, and peer interaction. Provide opportunities for students to work together on projects, group discussions, and problem-solving tasks.

7. Promote a Growth Mind-set: Foster a growth mind-set by emphasising the importance of effort, perseverance, and learning from mistakes. Encourage students to embrace challenges, view failures as learning opportunities, and develop a positive attitude towards their own growth and development.

8. Use Positive Reinforcement: Recognise and reinforce positive behaviour and achievements through verbal praise, written feedback, rewards, or other forms of acknowledgment. Focus on specific behaviours or efforts to encourage positive actions.

9. Implement Classroom Routines and Procedures: Establish consistent classroom routines and procedures that create a sense of structure and predictability. Clearly communicate and teach these routines to help students understand expectations and create an Organised and efficient learning environment.

10. Encourage Collaboration and Supportive Relationships: Foster a culture of collaboration and support among students. Teach and model teamwork, cooperation, and empathy. Encourage students to help and support one another academically and emotionally.

11. Create a Positive Physical Environment: Arrange the physical space in a way that promotes positive interactions, engagement, and comfort. Display student work, positive quotes, and inspirational visuals. Ensure that the classroom is Organised and inviting.

12. Reflect and Adjust: Regularly reflect on your classroom practices, seek feedback from students, and make adjustments as needed. Continuously improve your teaching strategies and approaches to enhance the classroom culture and meet the evolving needs of your students.

13. Provide Clear and Constructive Feedback: Give students timely and constructive feedback on their academic work and behaviour. Highlight their strengths and provide guidance for improvement. Encourage a growth mind-set by emphasising the importance of effort and learning from mistakes.

14. Teach and Model Social-Emotional Skills: Integrate social-emotional learning (SEL) activities into your curriculum. Teach and model skills such as empathy, active listening, conflict resolution, and self-regulation. Provide opportunities for students to practice these skills in real-life situations.

15. Reflect and Adjust: Regularly reflect on your classroom practices, seek feedback from students, and make adjustments as needed. Continuously improve your teaching strategies and approaches to enhance the classroom culture and meet the evolving needs of your students.

16. Create a Sense of Belonging: Foster a sense of belonging by creating classroom rituals, traditions, or activities that promote unity and a shared purpose. Encourage students to support and celebrate each other's successes and create a supportive and caring community.

Remember that creating a positive classroom culture is an ongoing process. Consistency, empathy, and a focus on building positive relationships are key. By implementing these strategies, you can create a classroom environment where students feel supported, motivated, and empowered to learn and thrive

What is a classroom culture?

Classroom culture refers to the shared values, beliefs, norms, attitudes, and behaviours that exist within a classroom community. It encompasses the overall atmosphere, interactions, and expectations that shape the learning environment. Classroom culture influences how students and educators interact, communicate, and engage in the learning process. It plays a crucial role in determining the overall dynamics, relationships, and effectiveness of teaching and learning.

A positive classroom culture fosters a supportive and inclusive environment where students feel safe, respected, and valued. It promotes collaboration, active participation, and a sense of belonging. In a positive classroom culture, students are encouraged to take risks, express their ideas, and engage in meaningful discussions. They feel empowered to ask questions, seek help, and actively contribute to their own learning.

A strong classroom culture is built upon the following elements:

Relationships and Respect:
Positive relationships between educators and students, as well as among students themselves, are fundamental to a healthy classroom culture. Respect for one another, empathy, and understanding create a supportive community where everyone feels valued.

Communication and Collaboration:
Effective communication and collaboration are essential in a positive classroom culture. Open lines of communication, active listening, and constructive feedback foster understanding, cooperation, and a sense of shared responsibility.

Engagement and Active Learning:
A positive classroom culture promotes active student engagement and meaningful learning experiences. Students are actively involved in discussions, hands-on activities, projects, and problem-solving tasks that enhance their understanding and critical thinking skills.

Inclusivity and Diversity:
A positive classroom culture embraces diversity and creates an inclusive environment where every student's voice is heard and respected. Differences are celebrated, and opportunities for cultural exchange and understanding are encouraged.

High Expectations and Support:
A positive classroom culture sets high expectations for academic achievement, behaviour, and personal growth. Educators provide necessary support, guidance, and resources to help students meet these expectations and reach their full potential.

Shared Responsibility and Ownership:

Students are encouraged to take ownership of their learning and contribute to the overall classroom culture. They have a voice in decision-making, participate in setting classroom norms and expectations, and play an active role in creating a positive learning environment.
Continuous Improvement and Reflection:
A positive classroom culture values reflection and continuous improvement. Educators and students reflect on their progress, identify areas for growth, and adapt their practices to enhance teaching and learning experiences.

Educators play a significant role in shaping the classroom culture through their interactions, instructional strategies, and classroom management practices. By intentionally fostering a positive classroom culture, educators create an environment that supports student success, well-being, and lifelong learning

Reflection and self-assessment,

Educators use a variety of techniques to teach students reflection and self-assessment skills. Here are some common methods employed by educators:

1. Model Reflection: Educators demonstrate the process of reflection by sharing their own thoughts and experiences. They might narrate their thinking process aloud or provide written examples of self-reflection. By modelling reflection, educators show students what it looks like and how it can be beneficial.

2. Guided Questions: Educators ask thought-provoking questions to help students reflect on their learning experiences. These questions encourage students to think deeply about what they have learned, how they have grown, and what they could do differently next time. Examples include: "What challenges did you face during this project?" or "How did your understanding change after completing this assignment?"

3. Learning Journals or Reflection Logs: Educators encourage students to keep journals or reflection logs to document their thoughts and experiences. Students can use these journals to write about their learning process, analyse their strengths and weaknesses, and set goals for improvement. Educators may review and provide feedback on these journals to facilitate further reflection.

4. Peer Feedback and Self-Assessment: Educators promote peer feedback and self-assessment practices, where students review their own work or provide feedback to their classmates. This process allows students to reflect on their own strengths and areas for growth while developing a deeper understanding of the criteria for success.

5. Group Discussions and Debates: Educators facilitate group discussions and debates that encourage students to articulate their thoughts, challenge assumptions, and critically analyse their own perspectives. These discussions provide opportunities for students to reflect on their own beliefs, consider alternative viewpoints, and refine their thinking.

6. Rubrics and Checklists: Educators provide students with rubrics or checklists that outline criteria for success. These tools help students assess their own work against specific standards or benchmarks. Students can use these resources to reflect on their progress and identify areas for improvement.

7. Goal Setting: Educators guide students in setting realistic and achievable goals. By helping students identify areas for growth, educators encourage self-assessment and reflection as students work towards their goals. Educators may provide guidance on setting measurable objectives and assist students in monitoring their progress.

8. Reflection Prompts and Worksheets: Educators provide reflection prompts or worksheets that guide students through a structured reflection process. These prompts

may focus on specific aspects of learning, such as content knowledge, problem-solving skills, or collaboration. Worksheets can help students Organise their thoughts and engage in meaningful reflection.

9.   Formative Assessment Strategies: Educators incorporate formative assessments throughout the learning process to gather feedback on student progress. By providing timely and constructive feedback, educators encourage students to reflect on their work, identify areas for improvement, and make necessary adjustments.

10.   Individual Conferences: Educators hold one-on-one conferences with students to discuss their progress, strengths, and areas for growth. These conferences provide a dedicated space for reflection and self-assessment. Educators offer personalised feedback, help students set goals, and collaborate on strategies for improvement.

Educators often use a combination of these techniques to foster reflection and self-assessment skills in their students. The specific methods employed may vary depending on the grade level, subject, and individual teaching style

Reflection Prompt Sheet

What is a reflection prompt sheet?

A reflection prompt sheet is a tool or document that provides students with specific questions or prompts to guide their reflective thinking. It serves as a structured framework to help students reflect on their learning experiences, achievements, challenges, and areas for improvement. Reflection prompt sheets typically contain a list of thought-provoking questions related to a particular topic, assignment, or learning objective.

Here's an example of what a reflection prompt sheet might look like:

1. Describe the task or project you worked on.
2. What were your initial thoughts or feelings about the task?
3. What strategies or approaches did you use to complete the task?
4. What was the most challenging part of the task? How did you overcome it?
5. Reflect on your strengths during the task. How did they contribute to your success?
6. Identify areas where you struggled or could have improved. What could you have done differently?
7. Did you face any obstacles or setbacks? How did you handle them?
8. What did you learn from completing this task? How has it contributed to your overall growth?
9. How does this task connect to your prior knowledge or experiences?
10. What goals or areas for improvement have you identified based on this task?

The prompts on the sheet encourage students to think critically about their learning process, analyse their performance, and consider strategies for future improvement.

Reflection prompt sheets can be tailored to specific subjects, projects, or learning objectives, allowing students to engage in targeted and meaningful self-reflection.

Educators may provide these sheets as handouts or include them in digital learning platforms for students to access and complete. They can also be used during individual conferences or as part of a larger reflective activity, such as portfolio assessments or end-of-unit reflections.

What is included in a student's self-assessment worksheet?

A student self-assessment worksheet typically includes various sections or components that allow students to reflect on their own learning, progress, and skills. Here are some common elements that can be included in a student self-assessment worksheet:

1. Learning Goals: Provide space for students to revisit the learning goals or objectives of a specific assignment, project, or unit. This allows students to reflect on their understanding of the intended outcomes.

2. Criteria for Success: Include a section that outlines the criteria for success or rubric for the task at hand. This helps students assess their work against specific standards or expectations.

3. Reflection Prompts: Include a series of thought-provoking questions or prompts that encourage students to think deeply about their learning process, strengths, challenges, and areas for improvement. These prompts should be relevant to the task or learning objective.

4. Self-Assessment Rating Scale: Offer a rating scale or checklist that allows students to assess their own performance or progress. This can be in the form of a numerical scale, checkmarks, or descriptive levels such as "exceeding expectations," "meeting expectations," or "below expectations."

5. Strengths and Achievements: Provide space for students to reflect on their strengths, accomplishments, or areas where they have demonstrated notable growth. This section allows students to acknowledge and celebrate their successes.

6. Areas for Improvement: Allocate a section where students can identify specific areas where they feel they need improvement or additional support. This self-reflection helps students recognise their weaknesses and focus on areas that require further attention.

7. Action Plan: Include a section for students to outline concrete steps they plan to take to address their areas for improvement. This can include setting goals, identifying resources or strategies, and planning next steps.

8. Teacher Feedback: Allocate space for students to review and respond to any feedback provided by the teacher. This provides an opportunity for students to reflect on the feedback, ask clarifying questions, or provide additional context.

9. Reflection Summary: Provide a section for students to summarise their overall reflections and takeaways from the self-assessment process. This can include insights gained, changes in perspective, or strategies they plan to implement moving forward.

The design and structure of a student self-assessment worksheet can vary depending on the grade level, subject, and specific learning context. It should be clear, Organised, and aligned with the goals of the assignment or learning activity. The worksheet should encourage students to engage in honest self-reflection and promote a growth mind-set by focusing on both strengths and areas for improvement.

Cultural sensitivity in the classroom

Educators play a crucial role in fostering cultural sensitivity in the classroom. Here are some strategies they can employ to ensure a culturally sensitive learning environment:

Educate Themselves: Educators should continuously educate themselves about different cultures, traditions, and perspectives. They can attend workshops, engage in professional development, read relevant literature, and seek out resources to deepen their understanding of cultural diversity.

Respect and Value Differences: Educators should actively promote respect and value the diverse backgrounds, experiences, and perspectives of their students. They can create a classroom culture that celebrates and appreciates cultural differences, fostering an inclusive and accepting environment.

Culturally Responsive Teaching: Employ culturally responsive teaching strategies that acknowledge and incorporate the cultural backgrounds and experiences of students into the curriculum. This can include incorporating culturally diverse materials, examples, and perspectives into lessons, making connections to students' lived experiences, and providing opportunities for students to share their own cultural knowledge.

Create a Safe and Inclusive Environment: Establish classroom norms and rules that promote respect, inclusivity, and open dialogue. Educators should actively address any form of discrimination, bias, or stereotypes that arise in the classroom. Encourage students to express their ideas, ask questions, and share their cultural experiences without fear of judgment or ridicule.

Incorporate Multicultural Content: Integrate multicultural content and resources into the curriculum. This can include literature, historical perspectives, art, music, and current events from a variety of cultures and backgrounds. Ensure that the materials selected are accurate, authentic, and free from stereotypes.

Engage in Cross-Cultural Communication: Encourage open and respectful communication among students from different cultural backgrounds. Provide opportunities for students to engage in meaningful discussions, share their experiences, and learn from one another's perspectives. Teach and model active listening skills and empathy to promote understanding and dialogue.

Use Culturally Sensitive Language: Be mindful of the language used in the classroom and ensure it is inclusive, respectful, and free from stereotypes or biases. Avoid making assumptions about students based on their cultural backgrounds and encourage others to do the same.

Individualised Support: Recognise that each student has unique cultural backgrounds, learning styles, and needs. Provide individualised support to students who may require additional assistance in navigating the curriculum, language challenges, or cultural transitions.

Collaborate with Families and Communities: Foster strong partnerships with families and communities by involving them in the education process. Engage in open communication with parents and caregivers to understand cultural values, traditions, and educational expectations. Involve families and community members in classroom activities, events, and celebrations to create a sense of belonging.

Reflect and Adapt: Regularly reflect on teaching practices and classroom dynamics to ensure cultural sensitivity. Seek feedback from students, families, and colleagues to continuously improve cultural responsiveness in the classroom. Adjust instructional strategies, materials, and approaches as needed to better meet the diverse needs of students.

By implementing these strategies, educators can create an inclusive and culturally sensitive learning environment that values and respects the diversity of their students

To address diverse learning styles in the classroom, educators can employ various strategies and techniques. Here are some ways educators can use diverse learning styles:

Differentiated Instruction: Educators can design and deliver instruction that caters to different learning styles. This involves providing multiple avenues for students to access and demonstrate their understanding of the content. For example, incorporating visual aids, hands-on activities, group discussions, and multimedia resources can accommodate diverse learning preferences.

Varied Instructional Materials: Educators can utilise a range of instructional materials, such as textbooks, videos, online resources, manipulatives, and real-world examples. By presenting information in different formats, educators can engage students with diverse learning styles, including visual, auditory, kinaesthetic, and tactile learners.

1. Cooperative Learning: Group activities and collaborative projects allow students to learn from each other, benefitting those who thrive in social settings. Cooperative learning also encourages teamwork, communication, and the development of interpersonal skills.

2. Multisensory Approaches: Incorporating multisensory activities engages multiple senses, which can be beneficial for students with different learning styles. Educators can integrate elements such as hands-on experiments, role-playing, demonstrations, and interactive technology to enhance learning experiences.

3. Flexible Instructional Strategies: Educators can offer choices and flexibility within their lessons to accommodate diverse learning styles. For instance, allowing students to choose between written assignments, oral presentations, or visual projects enables them to showcase their understanding in a way that aligns with their preferred learning style.

4. Individualised Support: Recognising that each student has unique learning preferences, educators can provide individualised support. This might involve offering additional resources, providing one-on-one guidance, or adapting instructional materials to better meet the needs of individual students.

5. Formative Assessment: Educators can use formative assessments, such as quizzes, discussions, and hands-on activities, to gauge student understanding and adapt instruction accordingly. This allows them to provide timely feedback and tailor their teaching approaches to address individual learning styles.

6. Learning Stations or Centres: Setting up different learning stations or centres within the classroom provides students with the opportunity to engage in various activities that cater to different learning styles. These stations can include independent reading, hands-on experiments, multimedia exploration, and collaborative projects.

7. Visual Aids and Graphic Organisers: Utilising visual aids, such as charts, diagrams, infographics, and graphic Organisers, can support visual learners by Organising and presenting information in a visually appealing and accessible format.

8. Reflection and Self-Assessment: Encouraging students to reflect on their own learning processes and preferences allows them to understand their own learning style better. Educators can guide students in identifying their strengths and weaknesses and help them develop strategies to leverage their learning style effectively.

By incorporating these strategies, educators can create an inclusive learning environment that embraces and supports diverse learning styles, allowing students to thrive and reach their full potential.

ISBN: 9798872216605   A.M. McIlwraith. FAIBHS., D.S.Ch.   Page 82

Differentiated assessment methods

Educators use differentiated assessment methods to accommodate the diverse needs, abilities, and learning styles of their students. Here are some strategies that educators can employ:

Varied Assessment Formats: Provide a range of assessment formats to cater to different learning styles and preferences. This can include written assignments, oral presentations, group projects, multimedia presentations, portfolios, performances, or a combination of these methods. By offering choices, students can demonstrate their understanding in a format that aligns with their strengths and learning style.

Flexible Response Options: Offer flexibility in response options to allow students to showcase their knowledge and skills in different ways. For example, instead of a traditional written test, provide alternatives such as creating a video, designing a visual representation, or participating in a debate or discussion. This allows students to leverage their strengths and engage in assessment tasks that best suit their abilities.

Adjusted Timeframes: Consider individual student needs and provide extended timeframes for completing assessments when necessary. Some students may require additional time to process information, Organise their thoughts, or demonstrate their understanding. By offering extended deadlines, educators ensure that all students have an equitable opportunity to complete assessments successfully.

Accommodations and Modifications: Make appropriate accommodations or modifications for students with specific learning needs. This may include providing additional resources, adjusting the complexity of the task, altering the format, or providing scaffolding and support. Accommodations and modifications ensure that students with diverse learning needs can access and demonstrate their knowledge effectively.

Rubrics and Criteria: Develop clear and specific rubrics or criteria that align with the learning objectives of the assessment. This helps students understand the expectations and criteria for success, regardless of the format or response option they choose. Rubrics can be tailored to accommodate different assessment methods and provide students with a clear understanding of what is being assessed.

Formative Assessment Strategies: Utilise a variety of ongoing formative assessment strategies to gather information about student progress and understanding. These can include observation, questioning techniques, self-assessments, peer assessments, and quizzes. Formative assessments provide valuable feedback to inform instruction and allow for adjustments and differentiation based on individual student needs.

Individual Conferences: Engage in one-on-one conferences with students to discuss their progress, understanding, and goals. Individual conferences offer an opportunity to provide personalised feedback, address misconceptions, and offer guidance for improvement. This tailored approach allows educators to meet the unique needs of each student.

Authentic Assessments: Incorporate authentic assessments that connect to real-world contexts and tasks. Authentic assessments require students to apply their knowledge and skills in meaningful ways. This can include projects, simulations, case studies, or problem-solving tasks that reflect the skills and knowledge students will need beyond the classroom.

Peer and Self-Assessment: Encourage students to engage in peer and self-assessment processes. Peer assessment involves students providing feedback and evaluating each other's work based on predetermined criteria. Self-assessment prompts students to reflect on their own learning, strengths, and areas for improvement. These processes promote metacognitive skills and allow students to take ownership of their learning.

Continuous Monitoring and Adjustments: Continuously monitor student progress and understanding throughout the assessment process. Make adjustments as needed to address individual needs, provide additional support, or challenge students who have already mastered the content. Regular monitoring helps ensure that assessments are responsive to student learning and facilitate growth.

By employing differentiated assessment methods, educators can gather comprehensive evidence of student learning and provide equitable opportunities for all students to demonstrate their knowledge, skills, and understanding in ways that best suit their individual needs and learning styles

How do educators integrate real-world examples into the learning plan?

Integrating real-world examples into the learning plan helps students connect their classroom learning to practical, everyday situations. Here are some strategies educators can use to incorporate real-world examples:

1. Case Studies: Use case studies that reflect real-life scenarios related to the topic being taught. Students can analyse the situations, apply their knowledge and problem-solving skills, and develop practical solutions. Case studies provide a context for students to understand the relevance and application of the concepts they are learning.

2. Guest Speakers and Experts: Invite guest speakers or subject matter experts to share their real-world experiences and insights related to the topic. They can provide first-hand accounts, demonstrate practical applications, and answer students' questions. Guest speakers bring authenticity and expertise to the classroom, making the learning experience more tangible and relevant.

3. Field Trips and Experiential Learning: Organise field trips or experiential learning opportunities that allow students to directly engage with real-world contexts. This can include visiting museums, businesses, laboratories, community Organisations, or natural environments. By immersing themselves in authentic settings, students can observe, collect data, and make connections between classroom content and the real world.

4. Current Events and News: Incorporate current events and news articles into lesson plans to illustrate how concepts and theories are applied in real-world contexts. Educators can facilitate discussions and analysis of news stories, encouraging students to critically evaluate the relevance and impact of what they are learning in their daily lives.

5. Project-Based Learning: Design project-based learning experiences where students tackle authentic problems or challenges. This approach allows students to apply their knowledge and skills to address real-world issues. Students can conduct research, design solutions, and present their findings, creating a tangible connection between their learning and real-life situations.

6. Role-Play and Simulations: Engage students in role-playing activities or simulations that simulate real-world scenarios. For example, students can take on different roles in a mock trial, a business negotiation, or a historical re-enactment. Role-playing allows students to step into real-world situations, experience decision-making, and understand the consequences of their actions.

7. Use Real-Life Data: Incorporate real-life data and statistics into lessons. Educators can provide students with authentic data sets related to the topic and guide them in analysing

and interpreting the data. This allows students to see how the concepts they are learning are applied and represented in real-world contexts.

8. Authentic Assessments: Design assessments that require students to apply their learning to real-world problems or tasks. This can include creating presentations, developing proposals, writing reports, or designing experiments. Authentic assessments reflect how knowledge and skills are utilised in real-life situations, providing students with meaningful opportunities to demonstrate their understanding.

9. Community Connections: Establish connections with local businesses, community Organisations, or experts in relevant fields. Collaborate with these external stakeholders to develop learning opportunities for students, such as mentorships, internships, or service-learning projects. By working with community partners, students can apply their learning in practical settings and gain a deeper understanding of real-world applications.

10. Reflection and Discussion: Encourage students to reflect on how the concepts they are learning connect to real-world contexts. Engage them in classroom discussions and reflections where they can share their thoughts, insights, and connections between theory and practice. This process helps students make meaningful connections and reinforces the relevance of their learning.

By integrating real-world examples into the learning plan, educators help students see the practical applications and relevance of their knowledge and skills. This approach fosters deeper understanding, engagement, and prepares students for real-world challenges and opportunities

Challenges and opportunities.

How do educators Foster curiosity and a love of learning in their students
Fostering curiosity and a love of learning in students is essential for their long-term engagement and success. Here are some strategies that educators can employ:

Create a Positive Learning Environment:
Establish a positive and inclusive classroom environment where students feel safe to ask questions, take risks, and explore their interests. Encourage a growth mind-set, emphasising that mistakes are opportunities for learning and growth.

Be a Role Model:
Demonstrate your own curiosity and enthusiasm for learning. Share your passion for the subject matter and model lifelong learning by showcasing your own love for acquiring knowledge. Your enthusiasm can be contagious and inspire students to develop their own curiosity.

Inquiry-Based Learning:
Incorporate inquiry-based approaches into your teaching, where students actively explore and investigate topics of interest. Encourage questioning, critical thinking, and problem-solving. Provide opportunities for students to conduct research, design experiments, and pursue independent inquiries.

Choice and Autonomy:
Offer students choices and autonomy in their learning. Provide options for topics, projects, or assignments, allowing students to pursue their interests and engage with the content in a personally meaningful way. Choice empowers students and fosters intrinsic motivation.

Hands-On Experiences:
Incorporate hands-on activities and real-world applications of the subject matter. Engage students in experiments, simulations, field trips, or projects to give them time to apply their learning in practical contexts. Hands-on experiences ignite curiosity and create memorable learning moments.

Connect to Students' Interests:
Relate the curriculum to students' interests, experiences, and real-life examples. Help students understand the relevance of what they are learning to their lives. Incorporate culturally diverse perspectives and examples that resonate with students.

Encourage Questions and Wondering:
Create a classroom culture that encourages questioning and wondering. Value all students' questions and provide meaningful responses. Foster an environment where students feel comfortable expressing curiosity and seeking answers.

Engage with Authentic Materials:

Utilise authentic and engaging materials, such as primary sources, current articles, videos, and real-world examples. These resources spark curiosity, invite exploration, and connect learning to the world beyond the classroom.

Promote Collaboration and Discussion:
Encourage collaboration and peer-to-peer learning. Facilitate discussions that allow students to share their ideas, ask questions, and engage in critical thinking. Create opportunities for students to learn from each other's experiences and perspectives.

Celebrate and Showcase Learning:
Recognise and celebrate students' achievements and growth. Showcase their work through presentations, exhibitions, displays, or performances. Publicly acknowledge their efforts and encourage them to take pride in their learning.

Provide Feedback and Support:
Offer constructive feedback that focuses on students' effort, progress, and areas for improvement. Support students in setting goals, developing strategies, and monitoring their own learning progress. Help them see the value of learning as a continuous process.

By implementing these strategies, educators can create an environment that nurtures curiosity and a love of learning in their students. By fostering a sense of wonder, intrinsic motivation, and personal relevance, educators can inspire students to become lifelong learners who are curious, engaged, and passionate about acquiring knowledge

Fostering curiosity and a love of learning in students is essential for their long-term engagement and success. Here are some strategies that educators can employ:

Create a Positive Learning Environment: Establish a positive and inclusive classroom environment where students feel safe to ask questions, take risks, and explore their interests. Encourage a growth mind-set, emphasising that mistakes are opportunities for learning and growth.

Be a Role Model: Demonstrate your own curiosity and enthusiasm for learning. Share your passion for the subject matter and model lifelong learning by showcasing your own love for acquiring knowledge. Your enthusiasm can be contagious and inspire students to develop their own curiosity.

Inquiry-Based Learning: Incorporate inquiry-based approaches into your teaching, where students actively explore and investigate topics of interest. Encourage questioning, critical thinking, and problem-solving. Provide opportunities for students to conduct research, design experiments, and pursue independent inquiries.

Choice and Autonomy: Offer students choices and autonomy in their learning. Provide options for topics, projects, or assignments, allowing students to pursue their interests and engage with the content in a personally meaningful way. Choice empowers students and fosters intrinsic motivation.

Hands-On Experiences: Incorporate hands-on activities and real-world applications of the subject matter. Engage students in experiments, simulations, field trips, or projects that allow them to apply their learning in practical contexts. Hands-on experiences ignites curiosity and create memorable learning moments.

Connect to Students' Interests: Relate the curriculum to students' interests, experiences, and real-life examples. Help students understand the relevance of what they are learning to their lives. Incorporate culturally diverse perspectives and examples that resonate with students.

Encourage Questions and Wondering: Create a classroom culture that encourages questioning and wondering. Value all students' questions and provide meaningful responses. Foster an environment where students feel comfortable expressing curiosity and seeking answers.

Engage with Authentic Materials: Utilise authentic and engaging materials, such as primary sources, current articles, videos, and real-world examples. These resources spark curiosity, invite exploration, and connect learning to the world beyond the classroom.

Promote Collaboration and Discussion: Encourage collaboration and peer-to-peer learning. Facilitate discussions that allow students to share their ideas, ask questions, and engage in critical thinking. Create opportunities for students to learn from each other's experiences and perspectives.

Celebrate and Showcase Learning: Recognise and celebrate students' achievements and growth. Showcase their work through presentations, exhibitions, displays, or performances. Publicly acknowledge their efforts and encourage them to take pride in their learning.

Provide Feedback and Support: Offer constructive feedback that focuses on students' effort, progress, and areas for improvement. Support students in setting goals, developing strategies, and monitoring their own learning progress. Help them see the value of learning as a continuous process.

ISBN: 9798872216605   A.M. McIlwraith. FAIBHS., D.S.Ch.   Page 90

To encourage critical reflection in students, educators can employ various strategies that promote deep thinking and self-analysis. Here are some approaches:

1. Thought-Provoking Questions: Pose open-ended and thought-provoking questions that require students to think critically and reflect on their learning experiences. These questions should go beyond simple recall and encourage students to analyse, evaluate, and synthesize information. Examples include: "Why do you think this problem occurred?" or "What are the implications of this historical event on today's society?"

2. Reflection Journals or Logs: Encourage students to keep reflection journals or logs where they can regularly document their thoughts, insights, and reflections on their learning. Provide prompts or guiding questions to help students delve deeper into their experiences and encourage critical thinking about their growth, challenges, and successes.

3. Socratic Discussions: Engage students in Socratic discussions, which involve questioning, challenging assumptions, and critically examining different perspectives. Encourage students to support their ideas with evidence and engage in respectful debates. Educators can guide the discussion and help students explore complex issues from multiple angles.

4. Peer Feedback and Self-Assessment: Foster a culture of peer feedback and self-assessment. Encourage students to provide constructive feedback to their peers, promoting critical reflection on their own work and that of their classmates. Self-assessment prompts students to evaluate their own strengths, weaknesses, and areas for growth, encouraging metacognition and critical analysis of their learning.

5. Analysing and Evaluating Information: Teach students to critically analyse and evaluate information from various sources. Guide them in considering the credibility, bias, and reliability of information, and encourage them to question assumptions and seek evidence. Help students develop the skills to distinguish fact from opinion and critically assess the quality of arguments.

6. Problem-Based Learning: Engage students in problem-based learning activities where they encounter real-world problems or challenges. Encourage them to think critically and reflect on potential solutions, considering multiple perspectives and analysing the implications of their proposed actions.

7. Reflective Assessments: Design assessments that require students to reflect critically on their learning and provide evidence of their understanding. This can include reflective essays, portfolios, presentations, or projects that prompt students to analyse their growth, evaluate their progress, and articulate their metacognitive processes.

8.   Metacognitive Strategies: Teach metacognitive strategies explicitly, such as setting goals, monitoring progress, and reflecting on learning strategies. Encourage students to think about their own thinking (metacognition) and develop self-regulation skills. Help them recognise the importance of critical reflection in enhancing their learning outcomes.

9.   Real-World Connections: Connect classroom learning to real-world issues, current events, or personal experiences. Encourage students to critically reflect on how the concepts they are learning relate to the world around them. Promote discussions on the implications and applications of their learning in real-life contexts.

10.   Teacher Feedback: Provide timely and constructive feedback to students that encourage critical reflection. Offer specific comments that prompt students to analyse their work, consider alternative approaches, and identify areas for improvement. Encourage students to act upon feedback and revise their work based on critical reflection.

By implementing these strategies, educators can foster a culture of critical reflection in their students. By encouraging them to question, analyse, evaluate, and synthesize information, students develop critical thinking skills that are valuable in their academic pursuits and future endeavours

What strategies do educators use to promote teamwork and collaboration?

Educators can employ various strategies to promote teamwork and collaboration among students. Here are some effective approaches:

Establish a Positive Classroom Culture: Create a positive and inclusive classroom culture that values teamwork and collaboration. Set clear expectations for respectful communication, active listening, and valuing diverse perspectives. Foster a safe and supportive environment where students feel comfortable collaborating with their peers.

Cooperative Learning Activities: Incorporate cooperative learning activities that require students to work together towards a common goal. Assign group projects, problem-solving tasks, or discussions that encourage students to actively participate, contribute their unique strengths, and collaborate effectively.

Group Norms and Roles: Help students establish group norms and roles to ensure effective collaboration. Teach students how to collaborate successfully by assigning specific roles within groups, such as a facilitator, recorder, timekeeper, or encourager. Establish clear expectations for each role and encourage students to hold themselves and their peers accountable.

Structured Collaboration Techniques: Teach students structured collaboration techniques, such as Think-Pair-Share, Jigsaw, or Gallery Walk. These techniques provide clear guidelines for students to engage in discussions, share ideas, and build upon each other's contributions. Structured techniques ensure that all students have opportunities to participate and collaborate.

Problem-Based Learning: Implement problem-based learning activities that require students to work together to solve real-world problems or challenges. These activities promote collaboration, critical thinking, and communication skills as students brainstorm, plan, and execute solutions collectively.

Peer Feedback and Peer Assessment: Incorporate peer feedback and peer assessment activities where students provide constructive feedback to their peers. This process encourages students to engage in critical thinking, analyse their peers' work, and offer suggestions for improvement. Peer assessment fosters collaboration and promotes shared responsibility for learning outcomes.

Group Reflection and Debriefing: Provide time for group reflection and debriefing after collaborative activities. Encourage students to discuss what worked well, challenges they faced, and lessons they learned through collaboration. This reflection process helps students develop self-awareness, identify effective teamwork strategies, and make improvements for future collaborations.

Technology Tools for Collaboration: Utilise technology tools that facilitate collaboration and teamwork. Platforms such as Google Docs, Padlet, or collaborative project management tools enable students to collaborate in real-time, share ideas, and work together on digital projects.

Team-Building Activities: Conduct team-building activities at the beginning of the school year or whenever new groups are formed. These activities help students build trust, develop effective communication, and establish positive relationships within their teams. Team-building activities can be fun, interactive, and promote a sense of belonging and collaboration.

Celebrate Collaborative Achievements: Recognise and celebrate collaborative achievements in the classroom. Acknowledge groups that demonstrate effective teamwork, problem-solving, and positive collaboration. This can be done through praise, certificates, or showcasing group work in the classroom or school community.

By implementing these strategies, educators can foster a collaborative learning environment where students develop essential teamwork skills, learn from each other, and accomplish shared goals. Collaboration prepares students for future endeavours that require effective teamwork and equips them with skills necessary for success in various aspects of life

What strategies do educators use to help students Break down complex concepts?

Educators can use several strategies to help students break down complex concepts and make them more accessible. Here are some effective approaches:

1. Pre-Assessment: Conduct a pre-assessment to gauge students' prior knowledge and identify any existing misconceptions. This information helps educators tailor their instruction and focus on areas where students need the most support.

2. Chunking: Break down complex concepts into smaller, more manageable chunks. Present information in bite-sized portions and guide students through each step or component. This approach allows students to process and understand one aspect before moving on to the next, gradually building their understanding of the whole concept.

3. Visual Representations: Use visual representations, such as diagrams, flowcharts, concept maps, or graphic Organisers, to illustrate the components and relationships within complex concepts. Visuals can make abstract ideas more concrete and help students see the connections between different elements.

4. Analogies and Metaphors: Employ analogies and metaphors to relate complex concepts to more familiar or concrete ideas. Comparing a complex concept to something simpler or more relatable can help students grasp the underlying principles and transfer their understanding.

5. Scaffolded Instruction: Provide scaffolded instruction by offering support and guidance as students work through complex concepts. Begin with explicit instruction, modelling the process and thinking required. Gradually release responsibility to students, allowing them to practice and apply their understanding independently.

6. Hands-On Activities: Engage students in hands-on activities, experiments, or simulations that allow them to explore and experience the concepts in a tangible way. By manipulating objects or conducting experiments, students can develop a deeper understanding of complex concepts.

7. Multimodal Instruction: Use a variety of instructional approaches to cater to different learning preferences. Incorporate visual aids, auditory explanations, interactive technology, and kinaesthetic activities to accommodate diverse learning styles and reinforce understanding.

8. Questioning Techniques: Ask probing questions to guide students' thinking and encourage them to analyse and break down complex concepts. Use a combination of lower-level and higher-level questions to prompt students to explain, analyse relationships, and apply their knowledge.

9. Collaborative Learning: Encourage collaborative learning where students work together to break down complex concepts. Collaborative discussions, group problem-solving tasks, and peer teaching provide opportunities for students to share their understanding, clarify misconceptions, and learn from each other.

10. Formative Assessment and Feedback: Incorporate formative assessments throughout the learning process to monitor students' understanding. Provide timely and specific feedback that highlights areas of improvement and guides students in breaking down complex concepts. Adjust instruction based on assessment data to address individual needs.

By using these strategies, educators can help students navigate complex concepts, develop a deeper understanding, and build the necessary foundational knowledge to tackle more advanced topics. Breaking down complex concepts into manageable components empowers students to approach learning with confidence and make meaningful connections between different parts of their education

How is humour used appropriately in the classroom?

Humour can be a powerful tool in the classroom when used appropriately. Here are some ways in which educators can incorporate humour effectively:

Ice Breakers and Warm-ups: Begin class with a light-hearted ice breaker or warm-up activity that involves humour. This helps create a positive and relaxed atmosphere, setting the tone for an engaging and enjoyable learning experience.

Storytelling and Anecdotes: Incorporate humorous anecdotes or stories related to the subject matter to make it more relatable and engaging. Sharing personal or funny experiences can capture students' attention and generate interest in the topic.

Jokes and Puns: Integrate tasteful jokes or puns that are relevant to the content being taught. Humorous statements or wordplay can help students remember and make connections to the material.

Visual Humour: Use visuals, such as funny images, cartoons, or memes, to illustrate concepts or add humour to presentations. Visual humour can provide a light-hearted break while reinforcing key ideas.

Playful Instructional Techniques: Infuse humour into instructional techniques, such as using funny voices, incorporating gestures, or employing humorous examples and analogies. This can make the learning experience more enjoyable and memorable for students.

Classroom Management: Use humour to diffuse tension or redirect behaviour during classroom management situations. A well-timed light-hearted comment or humorous intervention can help maintain a positive classroom climate.

Parody and Satire: Introduce parody or satire in appropriate contexts to encourage critical thinking and analysis. Analysing humorous content can deepen understanding, challenge assumptions, and stimulate discussion.

Student Engagement and Participation: Encourage students to contribute humorously during class discussions, debates, or presentations. This promotes an inclusive and supportive classroom environment where humour is valued and celebrated.

Teacher-Student Relationship: Develop a positive teacher-student relationship by incorporating humour into interactions. Light-hearted banter, inside jokes, or humorous comments can foster rapport and make students feel more comfortable and connected.

Reflection and Metacognition: Use humour as a tool for reflection and metacognition. Encourage students to reflect on their learning experiences by using humour to highlight challenges, successes, or growth. This can help students develop a sense of humour about their own learning processes.

It's important to note that humour should always be used with sensitivity and respect. Educators should consider the diverse cultural backgrounds and individual sensitivities of their students to ensure that humour is inclusive and does not offend or marginalise anyone. Humour should also never be used to belittle or ridicule students. The appropriate use of humour enhances the learning environment, promotes engagement, and contributes to a positive and enjoyable classroom experience.

How do educators incorporate movement and kinaesthetic activities?

To incorporate movement and kinaesthetic activities in the classroom, educators can use various strategies that engage students physically and enhance their learning experience. Here are some approaches:

1. Brain Breaks: Integrate short movement breaks into the lesson to help students release energy and refocus their attention. These breaks can include stretching exercises, jumping jacks, dance routines, or quick physical games. Brain breaks can be especially beneficial during longer periods of seated instruction.

2. Kinaesthetic Learning Stations: Set up learning stations or centres where students can engage in hands-on, physical activities related to the lesson. Each station can offer a different kinaesthetic experience, such as building models, conducting experiments, or solving puzzles. This allows students to actively explore and manipulate concepts.

3. Role-Playing and Skits: Incorporate role-playing or skits to encourage students to act out scenarios, historical events, or literary scenes. This kinaesthetic approach allows students to embody characters, explore perspectives, and enhance their understanding of content through physical engagement.

4. Movement-Based Review Games: Design review games that involve physical movement. For example, create a game where students solve math problems by throwing a ball to each other or form teams for a scavenger hunt to find and answer questions placed around the classroom. These games make the review process interactive and engaging.

5. Physical Manipulatives: Use manipulatives, such as blocks, counters, or tangible objects, to support learning. Students can use these objects to represent concepts, solve problems, or engage in hands-on activities. For instance, they can use blocks to build models or use counters to practice math operations.

6. Dance and Movement Activities: Incorporate dance or movement activities to explore concepts or express understanding. Students can create choreography that represents historical events, scientific processes, or literary themes. This approach combines kinaesthetic learning with creativity and self-expression.

7. Outdoor Learning: Take advantage of outdoor spaces, when available, to conduct lessons or activities that involve movement. Students can engage in nature walks, observe scientific phenomena, or participate in physical education activities. Outdoor learning provides a fresh environment that stimulates physical and cognitive engagement.

8. Collaborative Movement Tasks: Assign group tasks that require physical collaboration and movement. For example, have students work together to solve a puzzle or complete a science experiment that involves physical manipulation or coordination. Collaborative movement tasks foster teamwork, communication, and problem-solving skills.

9. Incorporate Movement into Instruction: While delivering instruction, encourage students to stand up, stretch, or move periodically. This can be as simple as asking students to switch seats, perform gestures that represent concepts, or engage in brief physical movements that align with the content being discussed.

10. Student-Led Demonstrations: Encourage students to take turns leading physical demonstrations or experiments to showcase their understanding. This allows them to actively engage with the content and share their knowledge with their peers.

By incorporating movement and kinaesthetic activities, educators can cater to different learning styles, increase student engagement, and create a dynamic and interactive learning environment. These strategies enhance students' understanding, promote physical well-being, and make learning a more holistic and enjoyable experience.

What strategies do educators use to incorporate hands-on activities into lesson plans?

Educators can incorporate hands-on activities into their lesson plans using various strategies to engage students actively in the learning process. Here are some effective approaches:

1.   Experiments and Investigations: Design hands-on experiments or investigations that allow students to explore concepts, test hypotheses, and make observations. Provide materials and guidance for students to conduct experiments independently or in small groups. This approach fosters critical thinking, problem-solving, and data analysis skills.

2.   Model Building and Manipulation: Encourage students to construct models or manipulate physical objects to represent abstract concepts. This can include building structures, creating diagrams, or using manipulatives such as blocks, puzzles, or models. Hands-on modelling helps students visualise and understand complex ideas.

3.   Simulation and Role-Playing: Use simulations or role-playing activities to immerse students in real-world scenarios or historical events. Provide props, costumes, or digital simulations to create a realistic and interactive experience. Simulations promote active engagement, critical thinking, and understanding of different perspectives.

4.   Interactive Technology: Utilise interactive technology tools and applications that enable students to engage in virtual hands-on activities. This can involve virtual labs, simulations, or augmented reality experiences that provide opportunities for exploration and experimentation.

5.   Field Trips and Outdoor Learning: Plan field trips or outdoor learning experiences that allow students to connect classroom learning to real-world contexts. Visit museums, nature reserves, historical sites, or community Organisations related to the subject matter. Field trips provide hands-on learning opportunities and deepen understanding through first-hand experiences.

6.   Project-Based Learning: Incorporate project-based learning where students engage in long-term, hands-on projects to investigate, create, or solve real-world problems. Provide guidance, resources, and checkpoints throughout the project to ensure learning objectives are met. Projects foster collaboration, creativity, and critical thinking skills.

7.   Arts Integration: Integrate visual arts, performing arts, or creative expression into lessons to provide hands-on experiences. For example, students can create artwork, perform skits, or compose songs related to the content. Artistic activities engage multiple senses and help students make meaningful connections to the subject matter.

8.   Data Collection and Analysis: Engage students in collecting and analysing data through hands-on activities. This can include conducting surveys, measuring and recording

observations, or analysing real-world data sets. Students can use tools such as sensors, data loggers, or software applications to collect and analyse data.

9. Collaborative Problem-Solving: Design hands-on problem-solving tasks that require collaboration and teamwork. Students work together to solve puzzles, complete challenges, or design solutions to real-world problems. Collaborative problem-solving activities promote critical thinking, communication, and cooperation.

10. Reflective and Metacognitive Tasks: Include hands-on tasks that encourage reflection and metacognition. For example, students can create visual representations of their learning, design concept maps, or engage in journaling activities to reflect on their understanding, challenges, and growth.

By incorporating hands-on activities, educators provide students with opportunities to actively engage with the content, develop problem-solving skills, and deepen their understanding. These strategies promote a student-cantered learning environment where learners become active participants in their own education

What strategies do educators use to include Active reading strategies?

Educators can use various strategies to promote active reading and help students engage with the text more effectively. Here are some approaches:

1. Pre-Reading Activities: Before students begin reading, engage them in pre-reading activities that activate their prior knowledge and build curiosity. These activities can include discussions, brainstorming, predicting, or using graphic Organisers to connect prior knowledge to the text.

2. Questioning: Encourage students to ask questions before, during, and after reading. This helps them stay actively engaged with the text and promotes deeper comprehension. Educators can model effective questioning techniques and guide students in generating their own questions.

3. Annotation and Highlighting: Teach students how to annotate texts by underlining, highlighting, or jotting down notes in the margins. Annotation helps students interact with the text, identify important information, make connections, and record their thoughts and questions.

4. Think-Alouds: Model think-alouds to demonstrate the cognitive processes involved in reading. Verbalise your thoughts, predictions, connections, and interpretations as you read aloud. This helps students develop metacognitive awareness and apply similar strategies to their own reading.

5. Text Coding and Marking: Teach students to use specific symbols or codes to mark different types of information in the text. For example, they can use symbols to mark unfamiliar words, key ideas, supporting evidence, or personal connections. Text coding helps students actively engage with the content and facilitates later review or discussion.

6. Reciprocal Teaching: Implement reciprocal teaching, where students take turns assuming the role of the teacher. They predict, clarify, question, and summarise sections of the text. This cooperative learning strategy promotes active reading, metacognition, and collaborative discussion.

7. Graphic Organisers: Provide graphic Organisers, such as concept maps, storyboards, or Venn diagrams, to help students visually Organise information from the text. Graphic Organisers support active reading by facilitating connections, summarisation, and the identification of main ideas and supporting details.

8. Summarisation and Synthesis: Encourage students to summarise sections of the text or create brief summaries after completing a reading passage. This requires active

engagement, comprehension, and the ability to synthesize information. Students can share their summaries with peers or create visual representations of the main ideas.

9. Scaffolding Techniques: Use scaffolding techniques to support students in active reading. This can include providing guiding questions, sentence starters, or structured note-taking templates. Scaffolding helps students focus their reading, make connections, and develop their own reading strategies.

10. Post-Reading Discussions and Reflections: Engage students in post-reading discussions or reflections to deepen their understanding and promote critical thinking. Encourage them to share their interpretations, ask clarifying questions, and relate the text to their own experiences or other texts. This helps consolidate learning and develop higher-order thinking skills.

By incorporating these strategies, educators promote active reading, enhance comprehension, and foster critical thinking skills in their students. Active reading strategies empower students to interact with texts, make connections, and derive meaning from their reading experiences

By incorporating these strategies, educators promote active reading, enhance comprehension, and foster critical thinking skills in their students. Active reading strategies empower students to interact with texts, make connections, and derive meaning from their reading experiences.

How do educators teach students Effective note-taking techniques?

Educators can help students develop effective note-taking techniques through explicit instruction, modelling, and guided practice. Here are some strategies educators can use:

1. Provide Note-Taking Guidelines: Introduce students to the purpose and benefits of note-taking. Explain the importance of capturing key information, Organising ideas, and recording personal connections or questions. Establish clear guidelines for note-taking, such as using abbreviations, focusing on main ideas, and staying actively engaged with the material.

2. Model Note-Taking: Model effective note-taking strategies by thinking aloud as you take notes during lessons or presentations. Demonstrate how to identify main ideas, summarise information, and use abbreviations or symbols. Discuss your thought processes and decision-making while selecting relevant details to include in your notes.

3. Cornell Method: Teach students the Cornell method, a widely used note-taking system. Explain how to divide notes into three sections: a narrow left margin for cues or questions, a larger right section for main ideas and details, and a summary section at the bottom. Guide students in using this method to organise their notes effectively.

4. Structured Note-Taking Templates: Provide structured note-taking templates to help students Organise their notes. These templates can include headings, bullet points, or graphic Organisers tailored to the content being studied. Templates provide students with a framework for recording information systematically.

5. Highlighting and Underlining: Teach students how to use highlighting and underlining effectively. Emphasise the importance of selectively highlighting key information rather than overusing these techniques. Encourage students to underline or highlight essential concepts, supporting details, or unfamiliar vocabulary to enhance comprehension.

6. Summarisation: Emphasise the importance of summarising information while taking notes. Teach students how to condense complex ideas into concise summaries using their own words. Encourage them to focus on capturing the main ideas and supporting details rather than transcribing everything verbatim.

7. Abbreviations and Symbols: Introduce students to common abbreviations and symbols that can be used during note-taking. This helps them save time and capture information

efficiently. Model the use of abbreviations and symbols in your own notes and provide a reference guide for students to use.

8. Active Listening Strategies: Teach students active listening strategies to enhance their note-taking. Emphasise the importance of listening for key ideas, signals of importance (such as repetition or emphasis), and transitions between topics. Guide students in identifying and recording these elements in their notes.

9. Graphic Organisers: Integrate graphic Organisers or visual aids to support note-taking. Provide templates such as concept maps, timelines, or Venn diagrams to help students visually Organise information and make connections. Graphic Organisers can serve as a scaffold for note-taking, helping students' structure their thoughts effectively.

10. Peer Collaboration and Review: Encourage students to collaborate with peers to review and compare notes. This allows them to gain different perspectives, clarify understanding, and fill in any gaps in their own notes. Peer collaboration fosters active engagement and strengthens note-taking skills.

11. Regular Practice and Feedback: Provide opportunities for students to practice note-taking regularly. Offer feedback on their notes, focusing on strengths and areas for improvement. Encourage self-reflection and goal-setting to help students refine their note-taking skills over time.

By implementing these strategies, educators can help students develop effective note-taking techniques that enhance comprehension, Organisation, and retention of information. Effective note-taking skills support students' active engagement with the content and serve as valuable tools for studying and reviewing material

What skills do educators teach students in Setting and managing expectations?

Educators teach students several important skills in setting and managing expectations. These skills include:

1. Clear Communication: Educators help students develop effective communication skills to express their expectations clearly and understand the expectations set by others. Students learn how to articulate their needs, ask for clarification, and express their boundaries in a respectful manner.

2. Active Listening: Educators teach students the importance of active listening, which involves attentively and empathetically understanding others' expectations. Students learn to listen to instructions, feedback, and the perspectives of their peers, fostering better understanding and cooperation.

3. Goal Setting: Educators guide students in setting realistic and achievable goals. Students learn how to set specific, measurable, attainable, relevant, and time-bound (SMART) goals that align with their abilities and aspirations. Educators help them break down larger goals into smaller, manageable steps.

4. Self-Reflection: Educators encourage students to reflect on their own expectations and assess their progress. Students learn to evaluate their strengths, weaknesses, and areas for improvement. Self-reflection helps students adjust their expectations, set new goals, and monitor their own growth.

5. Time Management: Educators teach students the importance of setting expectations around time management. Students learn strategies for prioritising tasks, managing their time effectively, and meeting deadlines. They develop skills to estimate the time required for various activities and create schedules to ensure timely completion.

6. Accountability: Educators help students understand the concept of accountability and its role in setting and managing expectations. Students learn to take responsibility for their actions, commitments, and academic performance. They develop a sense of ownership and learn to follow through on their responsibilities.

7. Flexibility and Adaptability: Educators teach students to be flexible and adaptable in their expectations. Students learn to navigate changes, setbacks, and unexpected circumstances. They develop resilience, problem-solving skills, and the ability to adjust their expectations when necessary.

8. Collaboration and Cooperation: Educators guide students in setting expectations for collaboration and cooperation in group work or classroom settings. Students learn to

establish norms for respectful communication, active participation, and valuing diverse perspectives. They develop skills for effective teamwork and conflict resolution.

9.   Empathy and Respect: Educators foster a classroom culture of empathy and respect, where students learn to consider others' perspectives, feelings, and expectations. Students develop skills for empathy, active listening, and respecting the boundaries and expectations of their peers.

10.   Self-Advocacy: Educators empower students to advocate for themselves by setting and communicating their own expectations. Students learn to express their needs, seek support when necessary, and assert their boundaries in a respectful manner. They develop confidence in voicing their expectations and concerns.

By teaching these skills, educators help students navigate social interactions, academic settings, and personal growth. Students develop the ability to set realistic expectations for themselves and others, communicate effectively, and adapt to different situations. These skills are valuable for their academic success, interpersonal relationships, and overall well-being.

Structured learning environments

Creating a structured learning environment

Creating a structured learning environment is crucial for promoting a positive and effective classroom experience. Here are some strategies that educators can use to establish a structured learning environment:

1. Clear Expectations: Clearly communicate expectations regarding behaviour, academic standards, and classroom procedures. Establish consistent rules and routines to provide a structured framework for students to follow. Ensure that students understand and have access to these expectations through verbal communication, visual aids, or written guidelines.

2. Classroom Organisation: Arrange the physical space in a way that supports structure and order. Use clearly labelled storage areas for materials, maintain a neat and clutter-free environment, and provide designated spaces for different learning activities. Organised physical spaces contribute to a sense of structure and facilitate smooth transitions.

3. Daily Schedules and Routines: Develop and display a daily schedule that outlines the different activities and their designated time slots. Establish consistent routines for tasks such as entering the classroom, transitioning between activities, and packing up at the end of the day. Routines provide predictability and help students feel secure within the structure of the learning environment.

4. Clear Instructions and Procedures: Clearly articulate instructions and procedures for various classroom activities, assignments, and transitions. Break down complex tasks into clear steps, use visual aids or demonstrations when necessary, and provide examples to ensure students understand what is expected of them. Consistency in instruction and procedures promotes a structured learning environment.

5. Use of Visual Supports: Utilise visual supports such as charts, posters, or visual schedules to reinforce structure and assist students in understanding expectations. Visual aids can serve as reminders for routines, rules, and academic procedures, providing a visual framework for students to follow.

6. Consistent Behaviour Management: Implement a consistent behaviour management system that supports structure and accountability. Clearly communicate behaviour expectations, establish consequences and rewards, and provide consistent feedback. Ensure that consequences are fair, age-appropriate, and aligned with the established expectations.

7.   Regular Transitions and Pacing: Plan and manage transitions between activities smoothly to maintain a structured flow of the learning environment. Provide clear signals or cues to indicate when transitions are about to occur. Consider pacing lessons appropriately to maintain engagement and avoid students becoming restless or disengaged.

8.   Engage Students Actively: Keep students actively engaged in learning activities through a variety of instructional strategies. Incorporate hands-on activities, discussions, group work, and other interactive approaches that promote active participation and foster a structured yet engaging environment.

9.   Positive Teacher-Student Relationships: Build positive relationships with students based on mutual respect, trust, and support. Students feel more secure and connected in a structured environment when they have a positive rapport with their teacher. Foster open communication, active listening, and understanding to establish a positive learning environment.

10. Regular Reflection and Adjustments: Regularly reflect on the effectiveness of the structured learning environment and make adjustments as needed. Seek student feedback, evaluate instructional strategies, and consider individual student needs. Flexibility and adaptability are key in maintaining an environment that meets the evolving needs of the students.

By implementing these strategies, educators can create a structured learning environment that promotes order, engagement, and a positive classroom culture. A structured environment provides students with a sense of security, predictability, and clarity, allowing them to focus on their learning and thrive academically.

How do you Modify instruction for students with special needs

Modifying instruction for students with special needs involves adapting teaching strategies, materials, and assessments to meet their unique learning needs. Here are some approaches that can be used:

1. Individualised Education Plans (IEPs): Review and follow the student's IEP, which outlines their specific learning goals, accommodations, and modifications. Collaborate with the student's support team, including special education educators, therapists, and parents, to ensure effective implementation of the IEP.

2. Differentiated Instruction: Adjust instructional methods, materials, and content to accommodate diverse learning needs. Provide multiple means of representation, expression, and engagement to support students' individual strengths and challenges. Differentiate instruction through varied instructional techniques, resources, and scaffolding.

3. Visual Supports: Incorporate visual aids such as visual schedules, graphic Organisers, charts, and visual cues to reinforce concepts, facilitate understanding, and support communication. Visual supports can enhance comprehension, Organisation, and independence for students with special needs.

4. Multi-Sensory Approaches: Engage multiple senses in instruction by incorporating hands-on activities, manipulatives, real-life examples, and interactive technology. Utilise tactile, auditory, and visual modalities to reinforce learning and cater to different learning styles.

5. Assistive Technology: Integrate assistive technology tools, such as text-to-speech software, speech recognition programs, adaptive keyboards, or communication devices, to support students' access to information, communication, and participation in classroom activities.

6. Flexible Grouping: Consider student strengths, interests, and learning styles when grouping students for collaborative activities. Provide opportunities for small group work, peer tutoring, or one-on-one instruction to cater to individual needs and promote social interaction.

7. Extended Time: Allow additional time for completing tasks, assignments, or assessments, as needed. This accommodation helps students with special needs manage their pace, process information, and demonstrate their understanding without feeling rushed.

8. Chunking and Simplifying Information: Break down complex concepts or instructions into smaller, more manageable parts. Present information in a sequential and Organised manner, providing clear and concise directions. Use simplified language, visual aids, or concrete examples to enhance understanding.

9. Social-Emotional Support: Foster a supportive and inclusive classroom environment that promotes social-emotional well-being. Provide opportunities for self-regulation, emotional expression, and peer interaction. Implement strategies such as visual supports for emotions, calm-down corners, or check-in routines to support students' social-emotional needs.

10. Ongoing Assessment and Feedback: Continuously assess students' progress using a variety of assessment methods that align with their abilities. Provide constructive feedback that is specific, timely, and focuses on growth. Adjust instruction and supports based on assessment data to address individual needs effectively.

It is essential to consult with special education professionals, collaborate with the student's support team, and continuously communicate with parents or caregivers to ensure the appropriate modifications and accommodations are provided. Each student with special needs has unique requirements, so individualisation and flexibility are key in modifying instruction to optimise their learning outcomes

What tools and techniques do educators use for Monitoring student progress?

Educators use various tools and techniques to monitor student progress effectively. Here are some commonly used ones:

1. Formative Assessments: Employ formative assessments throughout instruction to gather ongoing information about students' understanding and progress. These assessments can take the form of quizzes, exit tickets, classroom discussions, observations, or quick checks for understanding. Formative assessments provide valuable feedback that helps educators make instructional decisions and identify areas where students may need additional support.

2. Summative Assessments: Administer summative assessments, such as end-of-unit tests or projects, to evaluate students' overall mastery of the content. Summative assessments provide a snapshot of students' learning at a particular point in time and help measure their progress toward learning goals.

3. Rubrics and Scoring Guides: Use rubrics and scoring guides to provide clear criteria and expectations for assignments and projects. These tools allow educators to assess student work consistently and objectively, providing specific feedback and identifying areas for improvement.

4. Checklists and Observations: Utilise checklists and observation notes to monitor student behaviours, participation, and engagement during classroom activities. These tools help track individual student progress and inform instructional adjustments or interventions.

5. Learning Logs and Journals: Incorporate learning logs or journals where students record their reflections, questions, and progress. These tools provide insight into students' thought processes, self-assessment, and metacognitive development. Educators can review these logs to monitor growth and offer targeted feedback.

6. Digital Assessment Tools: Leverage digital assessment platforms or software that allow for efficient tracking and analysis of student progress. These tools provide data and analytics that help identify trends, analyse performance, and individualise instruction based on the specific needs of students.

7. Portfolios: Implement student portfolios as a collection of work that demonstrates growth over time. Portfolios can include samples of student work, self-reflections, and assessments. Educators and students can review portfolios periodically to assess progress and set goals for improvement.

8. Observational Assessments: Observe students during classroom activities, group work, discussions, or presentations to gauge their understanding, skills, and behaviours.

Observational assessments provide valuable insights into students' progress, collaboration, and application of knowledge in authentic contexts.

9.   Peer and Self-Assessment: Encourage peer and self-assessment practices where students assess their own work or provide feedback to their peers. Peer and self-assessment promote student ownership of learning and help develop critical thinking skills.

10.   Progress Monitoring Tools: Utilise progress monitoring tools specifically designed to track student progress over time. These tools can include standardised assessments, benchmark assessments, or progress monitoring charts that allow for data-driven decision-making.

Educators should consider using a combination of these tools and techniques based on the specific learning goals, subject area, and individual student needs. Regular monitoring of student progress provides valuable insights for instructional planning, differentiation, and targeted support to ensure optimal learning outcomes.

How do educators Provide guidance on study skills

Educators can provide guidance on study skills to help students develop effective strategies for independent learning. Here are some approaches they can use:

1. Explicit Instruction: Provide direct instruction on various study skills and techniques. Explain the purpose and benefits of each skill, demonstrate how to use them effectively, and highlight their relevance to academic success.

2. Time Management: Teach students strategies for managing their time effectively. Help them create schedules, prioritise tasks, and allocate time for studying. Emphasise the importance of setting realistic goals and maintaining a balance between academic work and other activities.

3. Note-Taking Techniques: Teach students different note-taking methods such as Cornell notes, mind maps, or outlining. Explain when and how to use each technique based on the type of material being studied. Model effective note-taking strategies and provide opportunities for guided practice.

4. Active Reading Strategies: Teach students strategies to enhance their reading comprehension and engagement. These may include previewing the text, highlighting or underlining key information, annotating the text, and using questioning techniques to promote critical thinking.

5. Organisational Skills: Help students develop Organisational skills to manage their study materials and resources. Teach them how to keep track of assignments, create filing systems for handouts and notes, and maintain a well-Organised study area.

6. Test-Taking Strategies: Instruct students on effective test-taking strategies, such as reading instructions carefully, managing time during exams, and using techniques like process of elimination or educated guessing. Help students understand different question formats and how to approach them.

7. Memory Techniques: Introduce memory-enhancing strategies, such as mnemonics, visualisation, or chunking, to help students retain and recall information more effectively. Teach them how to use these techniques when studying or reviewing material.

8. Self-Reflection and Metacognition: Encourage students to reflect on their study habits and learning processes. Help them identify their strengths and areas for improvement. Teach metacognitive strategies, such as setting goals, monitoring progress, and adjusting study strategies based on self-assessment.

9.   Study Groups and Peer Collaboration: Promote the benefits of studying in groups or with peers. Encourage students to form study groups to review material, discuss concepts, and share knowledge. Teach them effective communication and collaboration skills within study group settings.

10.   Provide Resources and Tools: Share study resources and tools with students, such as study guides, graphic Organisers, or online resources. Recommend reliable websites, apps, or software that can support their independent learning and Organisation.

11.   Individualised Support: Recognise that students may have different learning styles and preferences. Provide individualised support by offering personalised recommendations based on students' strengths, challenges, and learning profiles. Offer one-on-one guidance and check-ins to address specific needs.

Educators should incorporate regular opportunities for students to practice and apply these study skills, providing feedback and reinforcement. They can also integrate study skills into subject-specific lessons to help students develop subject-specific study strategies. By providing guidance on study skills, educators empower students to become independent learners and equip them with essential tools for academic success.

What do educators do to ensure Effective use of praise and rewards?

To ensure the effective use of praise and rewards, educators can employ the following strategies:

1. Specific and Genuine Praise: Provide specific and meaningful praise that highlights the specific effort, improvement, or achievement demonstrated by the student. Acknowledge the specific behaviour or accomplishment and explain why it is praiseworthy. Ensure that praise is genuine and sincere.

2. Timeliness: Offer praise and rewards in a timely manner. Recognise and acknowledge students' efforts and achievements promptly to reinforce the connection between their actions and the positive feedback. Immediate recognition helps students understand the cause and effect relationship between their behaviour and the praise or reward.

3. Balance Intrinsic and Extrinsic Motivation: Encourage intrinsic motivation by highlighting the value and enjoyment of the learning process itself. Emphasise the satisfaction and sense of accomplishment that comes from mastering skills or achieving personal growth. While extrinsic rewards can be used selectively, educators should focus on fostering students' intrinsic motivation for long-term engagement and success.

4. Varied Forms of Rewards: Utilise a variety of rewards to cater to different student preferences and interests. These rewards can include verbal praise, written notes, certificates, privileges, small incentives, or opportunities for increased responsibility. Tailor rewards to align with individual student preferences and what is meaningful to them.

5. Progress-Oriented Feedback: Provide feedback that focuses on students' progress and effort rather than solely on the outcome or end result. Encourage a growth mind-set by praising students for their perseverance, problem-solving skills, or strategies used. This type of feedback fosters a sense of continuous improvement and resilience.

6. Individualisation: Recognise and appreciate students' unique strengths, talents, and accomplishments. Tailor praise and rewards to acknowledge the individual progress and achievements of each student. Avoid making comparisons or creating an overly competitive environment.

7. Opportunities for Self-Reflection: Encourage students to reflect on their own efforts and progress. Help them develop self-awareness by prompting them to recognise their strengths, areas of growth, and the strategies they used to succeed. Guide them in setting personal goals and recognising their own accomplishments.

8. Teach Peer Recognition: Foster a classroom culture where students recognise and appreciate one another's efforts and achievements. Promote peer-to-peer praise and recognition through structured activities, such as peer feedback, group reflections, or sharing success stories.

9. Use Praise as a Motivational Tool: Use praise strategically to motivate students and reinforce desired behaviours. Praise can be used to encourage positive classroom behaviours, academic engagement, collaborative teamwork, or the application of specific learning strategies. Use praise as a tool to shape behaviour and cultivate a positive classroom environment.

10. Relationship Building: Develop positive and respectful relationships with students. Build trust, establish rapport, and demonstrate genuine care for their well-being. When praise and rewards come from a trusted and supportive teacher-student relationship, they have a greater impact on student motivation and engagement.

By following these strategies, educators can ensure that praise and rewards are used effectively to motivate students, reinforce desired behaviours, and create a positive and supportive learning environment. The goal is to foster intrinsic motivation, build students' self-esteem, and encourage a growth mind-set for long-term success

How do educators Adapt instruction for different age groups

Adapting instruction for different age groups requires considering the developmental characteristics, abilities, and learning styles of students at each stage. Here are some general strategies educators can use:

1. Early Childhood (Preschool and Kindergarten):

    Utilise hands-on and play-based learning activities that engage the senses and promote exploration.

    Incorporate songs, rhymes, and stories to enhance language development and vocabulary.

    Provide opportunities for active movement and physical play to support gross and fine motor skill development.

    Use visual aids and concrete materials to support understanding of abstract concepts.

    Keep instructions simple and provide clear visual cues or demonstrations.

2. Elementary School:

    Use a variety of instructional methods to accommodate diverse learning styles, such as visual, auditory, and kinaesthetic.

    Incorporate interactive and collaborative activities to engage students in their learning.

    Provide opportunities for students to express their thoughts and ideas through discussions, writing, and presentations.

    Gradually introduce more complex and abstract concepts, building on students' prior knowledge and experiences.

    Offer a balance of structure and choice to foster independence and responsibility.

3. Middle School:

    Foster a supportive and inclusive classroom environment that acknowledges the social and emotional changes experienced by students at this age.

    Encourage active participation and critical thinking through debates, project-based learning, and problem-solving activities.

Provide opportunities for student choice and exploration within structured guidelines.

Use technology tools and multimedia resources to enhance engagement and facilitate research and presentation skills.

Support Organisational and study skills development to prepare students for increased academic demands.

4.   Post Primary School:
Offer a variety of instructional strategies that promote higher-order thinking skills, including analysis, synthesis, and evaluation.

Provide opportunities for student-driven inquiry, research, and independent projects.

Incorporate real-world connections and applications of knowledge to foster relevance and engagement.

Facilitate discussions and debates that encourage diverse perspectives and critical analysis.

Prepare students for education and careers by developing skills such as time management, collaboration, and research.

Remember that individual students within each age group may have different learning needs and abilities. Differentiation within age groups is essential to meet the diverse needs of students. Regular assessments, ongoing feedback, and building positive relationships with students can help educators tailor instruction to best support each learner.

What techniques do educators use to promote active learning?

Educators use various techniques to promote active learning in the classroom. Here are some effective strategies:

1.	Collaborative Learning: Encourage students to work together in pairs or small groups on projects, discussions, or problem-solving activities. Collaborative learning promotes active engagement, communication, and the exchange of ideas among students.

2.	Inquiry-Based Learning: Foster curiosity and critical thinking skills by posing open-ended questions or real-world problems that require students to investigate, analyse, and draw conclusions. Encourage students to ask questions, explore multiple perspectives, and seek solutions through inquiry.

3.	Problem-Based Learning: Present students with authentic, real-life problems or challenges that require them to apply their knowledge and skills to develop solutions. Guide students through the problem-solving process, providing support and facilitating reflection on their experiences.

4.	Project-Based Learning: Engage students in long-term, in-depth projects that allow them to explore topics of interest, apply knowledge, and demonstrate their understanding through hands-on activities, research, and presentations. Projects provide opportunities for active learning, creativity, and collaboration.

5.	Socratic Method: Use a question-and-answer approach inspired by Socrates to stimulate critical thinking and discussion. Ask thought-provoking questions that challenge students to analyse, evaluate, and articulate their ideas. Encourage students to engage in respectful debate and support their arguments with evidence.

6.	Flipped Classroom: Reverse the traditional model of instruction by having students engage with the content outside of class through videos, readings, or online resources. Classroom time is then dedicated to activities that promote active learning, such as discussions, problem-solving, or hands-on experiments.

7.	Think-Pair-Share: Pose a question or problem and give student's time to think individually. Then, have them pair up with a partner to discuss their thoughts and perspectives. Finally, facilitate a whole-class discussion to share and compare ideas.

8.	Role-Playing or Simulations: Engage students in role-playing activities or simulations that allow them to step into different roles, perspectives, or scenarios. This immersive approach promotes active learning, empathy, and the application of knowledge in practical contexts.

9. Peer Teaching: Encourage students to take on the role of a teacher by having them explain concepts, demonstrate processes, or lead discussions with their peers. Peer teaching enhances understanding, communication skills, and collaboration.

10. Hands-On Activities: Provide opportunities for hands-on learning through experiments, demonstrations, or manipulatives. Engage students in tactile experiences that connect abstract concepts to concrete examples.

11. Technology Integration: Incorporate educational technology tools, such as interactive presentations, simulations, or virtual reality, to enhance active learning. Technology can provide immersive and interactive experiences that promote engagement and understanding.

12. Reflection and Metacognition: Build in regular opportunities for students to reflect on their learning experiences, identify strengths and areas for improvement, and set goals for further learning. Promote metacognitive skills by encouraging students to monitor their thinking and adjust strategies as needed.

By implementing these strategies, educators can promote active learning, critical thinking, and student engagement. Active learning approaches foster deeper understanding, long-term retention of knowledge, and the development of essential 21st-century skills

How do educators get students to Demonstrate enthusiasm for the subject matter?

Educators can employ several strategies to help students demonstrate enthusiasm for the subject matter:

1. Personal Relevance: Connect the subject matter to students' lives and interests. Relate the content to real-world examples, current events, or personal experiences to show its relevance and practical applications. Help students see how the subject matter relates to their goals, passions, or future careers.

2. Authentic Learning Experiences: Provide opportunities for students to engage in hands-on, authentic learning experiences. Incorporate real-world projects, simulations, or field trips that allow students to apply their knowledge and skills in meaningful ways. Authentic experiences can spark enthusiasm by making the subject matter tangible and relevant.

3. Engaging Instructional Methods: Utilise varied and engaging instructional methods to capture students' interest and attention. Incorporate multimedia resources, technology tools, interactive activities, or demonstrations to make the learning experience more dynamic and enjoyable.

4. Student Choice and Voice: Give students opportunities to make choices about their learning within the subject matter. Offer options for research topics, project formats, or ways to demonstrate understanding. Providing autonomy and empowering students to have a voice in their learning can increase enthusiasm and ownership of the subject matter.

5. Active Participation and Collaboration: Encourage active participation and collaboration among students. Design activities that require students to work together, discuss ideas, or solve problems as a team. Create a supportive classroom environment that values student contributions and encourages participation.

6. Positive Teacher-Student Relationships: Build positive relationships with students by showing genuine care, respect, and enthusiasm for the subject matter. Share your own enthusiasm and passion for the content, and let students see your excitement. Create a positive and supportive classroom culture that fosters a love of learning.

7. Incorporate Novelty and Variety: Introduce novelty and variety into the learning experience to capture students' attention and maintain their interest. Use diverse instructional strategies, incorporate new resources or technologies, or introduce unexpected elements that surprise and engage students.

8. Celebrate Achievements: Recognise and celebrate students' achievements, progress, and growth in the subject matter. Provide positive feedback, acknowledge their efforts,

and publicly celebrate successes. This recognition and validation can foster enthusiasm and motivate students to continue their engagement.

9.   Share Enthusiasm-Inducing Resources: Share resources, such as books, articles, videos, or podcasts that showcase the excitement and possibilities within the subject matter. Expose students to inspiring role models, success stories, or real-life applications that ignite their enthusiasm.

10.   Foster Curiosity and Inquiry: Encourage students to ask questions, explore ideas, and pursue their own inquiries within the subject matter. Support their curiosity by creating a safe space for exploration and providing resources or guidance to pursue their interests.

11.   Emotional Connection: Help students develop an emotional connection to the subject matter by tapping into their emotions and values. Explore thought-provoking topics, use storytelling or personal narratives, and engage students in discussions that elicit emotional responses or highlight the subject's significance.

By implementing these strategies, educators can create an environment that nurtures students' enthusiasm for the subject matter. When students find joy, relevance, and personal meaning in what they are learning, they are more likely to demonstrate enthusiasm, engage deeply, and develop a lifelong love for the subject.

Teaching effective research skills is essential for empowering students to gather, evaluate, and utilise information effectively. Here are some strategies educators can use to teach these skills:

1. Introduction to Research Process: Provide an overview of the research process, including the steps involved (such as topic selection, information gathering, evaluation, and synthesis). Explain the importance of conducting thorough research and the value of reliable and credible sources.

2. Information Literacy: Teach students how to identify and access different types of information sources, including books, academic journals, websites, and databases. Emphasise the importance of evaluating the credibility, relevance, and currency of sources.

3. Search Strategies: Demonstrate effective search strategies for online research, including the use of keywords, advanced search operators, and filtering options. Introduce students to search engines and databases specific to their subject area.

4. Source Evaluation: Teach students how to critically evaluate sources for reliability, accuracy, bias, and relevance. Provide guidelines or checklists for assessing the credibility of sources, distinguishing between primary and secondary sources, and identifying reputable authors or publishers.

5. Note-Taking and Organisation: Guide students in developing effective note-taking techniques while conducting research. Teach them how to summarise information, paraphrase, and record proper citations. Emphasise the importance of Organising their notes and sources for easy retrieval.

6. Proper Citation and Avoiding Plagiarism: Instruct students on proper citation formats. Teach them how to give credit to the original authors or sources and avoid plagiarism. Introduce tools like citation generators or reference management software to facilitate the citation process.

7. Critical Analysis and Synthesis: Teach students to critically analyse and synthesize information gathered from multiple sources. Help them identify patterns, draw connections, and develop coherent arguments or viewpoints based on their research findings.

8. Ethical Use of Information: Discuss ethical considerations related to information use, copyright, and intellectual property. Teach students to respect copyright laws and to use information ethically and responsibly.

9. Collaborative Research: Provide opportunities for students to engage in collaborative research projects. Assign group research tasks, encourage peer feedback, and facilitate discussions where students can learn from each other's research experiences.

10. Reflection and Metacognition: Incorporate opportunities for students to reflect on their research process, challenges encountered, and lessons learned. Promote metacognitive awareness by having students identify their strengths and areas for improvement in conducting research.

11. Authentic Research Projects: Assign research projects that align with students' interests, allowing them to explore topics they are passionate about. Encourage independent inquiry and provide guidance as students conduct research on their chosen topics.

12. Ongoing Support and Feedback: Offer ongoing support and feedback throughout the research process. Provide guidance, answer questions, and offer constructive feedback on students' research proposals, search strategies, notes, and final projects.

By implementing these strategies, educators can equip students with the necessary research skills to navigate the vast amount of information available and critically evaluate and utilise it effectively. Effective research skills are essential not only for academic success but also for lifelong learning and informed decision-making.

Teaching effective presentation skills

Teaching effective presentation skills is important for helping students communicate their ideas confidently and effectively. Here are some strategies educators can use to teach these skills:

1. Modelling: Model effective presentation techniques by delivering engaging and well-structured presentations yourself. Demonstrate skills such as clear articulation, appropriate pacing, body language, and effective use of visual aids.

2. Presentation Structure: Teach students the importance of Organising their presentations with a clear introduction, main points, and a conclusion. Encourage them to use a logical flow and transitions between ideas to enhance coherence and understanding.

3. Audience Awareness: Emphasise the importance of considering the audience when preparing presentations. Discuss how to adapt content, language, and delivery to suit the needs and interests of the audience. Encourage students to anticipate and address potential questions or concerns.

4. Visual Design: Teach students how to create visually appealing and informative slides or visual aids. Discuss principles of design, such as using clear fonts, appropriate colours, and engaging visuals. Emphasise the importance of simplicity and avoiding overcrowded slides.

5. Verbal Communication: Help students develop their verbal communication skills by focusing on clarity, tone, and volume. Encourage them to practice using a confident and expressive voice, while avoiding common speech pitfalls like fillers or monotone delivery.

6. Body Language and Nonverbal Communication: Discuss the role of body language in effective presentations. Teach students techniques for maintaining eye contact, using appropriate gestures, and expressing confidence and engagement through posture and facial expressions.

7. Engaging Openings and Closings: Guide students on how to create engaging openings that capture the audience's attention and set the tone for the presentation. Teach them strategies for creating memorable closings, such as summarising key points or ending with a thought-provoking question.

8. Visualise Data and Statistics: Teach students how to effectively present data, charts, and statistics. Discuss techniques for visually representing information in a clear and concise manner. Encourage students to explain and interpret the data to make it meaningful to the audience.

9.   Practice and Rehearsal: Provide opportunities for students to practice their presentations before delivering them. Encourage them to rehearse their delivery, timing, and use of visual aids. Offer feedback and suggestions for improvement during practice sessions.

10.   Peer Feedback and Evaluation: Promote a culture of constructive feedback by incorporating peer evaluations of presentations. Encourage students to provide specific feedback on content, delivery, and visual aids. Teach them how to provide feedback respectfully and offer suggestions for improvement.

11.   Confidence Building: Help students build confidence in their presentation skills by providing positive reinforcement and creating a supportive classroom environment. Encourage them to focus on their strengths and improvement areas, celebrating progress along the way.

12.   Reflection and Self-Assessment: Incorporate opportunities for students to reflect on their presentation experiences. Encourage self-assessment, where students evaluate their own strengths, areas for improvement, and strategies they can employ in future presentations.

By implementing these strategies, educators can support students in developing effective presentation skills. These skills are essential for academic and professional success, as well as for effective communication in various settings. Offering guidance, practice, and feedback helps students build confidence, articulate their ideas with clarity, and engage their audience effectively

Effective test-taking strategies

Teaching effective test-taking strategies can help students approach exams with confidence, manage their time effectively, and demonstrate their knowledge and skills. Here are some strategies educators can use to teach these skills:

1.   Familiarise Students with Test Formats: Introduce students to different types of test formats they may encounter, such as multiple-choice, true/false, short answer, or essay questions. Discuss the purpose and expectations of each format, and provide examples for practice.

2.   Review Test-Taking Techniques: Teach students specific techniques for approaching different types of questions. For example, strategies such as process of elimination, educated guessing, or breaking down complex questions into manageable parts can be helpful. Provide practice opportunities for students to apply these techniques.

3.   Time Management: Teach students how to manage their time effectively during tests. Discuss the importance of reading instructions carefully, allocating time for each section or question, and budgeting time for review at the end. Encourage students to practice time management strategies during timed activities or practice tests.

4.   Active Reading and Skimming Techniques: Teach students how to skim passages or questions to gain a general understanding before diving into detailed reading. Highlight the importance of actively engaging with the text, underlining key information, and using context clues to answer questions effectively.

5.   Answering Multiple-Choice Questions: Guide students on how to approach multiple-choice questions, including techniques such as reading each option carefully, eliminating obviously incorrect answers, and using strategies to narrow down choices. Emphasise the importance of understanding the question stem and reading all options before selecting an answer.

6.   Effective Essay Writing: Provide guidance on structuring and Organising essay responses. Teach students how to analyse essay prompts, create outlines, develop a clear thesis statement, and support their arguments with relevant evidence or examples. Offer strategies for time management within the essay writing process.

7.   Test Anxiety Management: Address test anxiety by discussing relaxation techniques, deep breathing exercises, and positive self-talk. Teach students strategies to manage stress and stay focused during tests. Encourage them to develop effective study habits and practice self-care before exams.

8.   Practice and Review: Incorporate regular practice tests and quizzes to familiarise students with the testing process. Provide opportunities for students to review their answers and reflect on their performance. Discuss common mistakes or misconceptions to promote learning and growth.

9.

10.   Study Skills: Teach students effective study strategies, such as creating study guides, using mnemonic devices, Organising information visually, or practicing active recall. Help students develop personalised study plans that align with their learning style and preferences.

11.   Test-Taking Environment: Discuss the importance of creating a conducive test-taking environment, including minimising distractions, ensuring adequate lighting and comfortable seating, and encouraging a focused mind-set.

12.   Test-Taking Ethics: Promote integrity and ethical behaviour during tests. Discuss the importance of avoiding cheating, using unauthorised resources, or sharing answers with peers. Teach students the consequences of dishonesty and the value of their personal integrity.

13.   Reflection and Analysis: Provide opportunities for students to reflect on their test performance, identify areas for improvement, and develop strategies for future success. Encourage students to seek feedback from educators and use it to inform their test-taking strategies.

By incorporating these strategies into test preparation and instruction, educators can empower students with effective test-taking skills. These strategies can help students approach exams with greater confidence, reduce anxiety, and perform at their best.

Using case studies and real-life scenarios in teaching can provide valuable opportunities for students to apply their knowledge and skills in authentic contexts. Here are some strategies for incorporating case studies and real-life scenarios:

1. Select Relevant and Engaging Cases: Choose case studies or scenarios that are relevant to the subject matter and aligned with the learning objectives. Select cases that are engaging and capture students' interest, such as real-world examples, historical events, or current issues.

2. Introduce Background Information: Provide background information about the case or scenario to provide context and set the stage for analysis. Include relevant facts, data, or key concepts that students need to understand the situation.

3. Encourage Critical Thinking: Use case studies and scenarios to foster critical thinking skills. Ask open-ended questions that require analysis, evaluation, and problem-solving. Challenge students to consider multiple perspectives and apply their knowledge to propose solutions or make informed decisions.

4. Small Group Discussions: Divide students into small groups to discuss the case or scenario. Encourage active participation, collaboration, and the sharing of different perspectives. Students can exchange ideas, debate solutions, and collectively work towards a deeper understanding of the subject matter.

5. Analyse and Evaluate: Guide students to analyse and evaluate the case or scenario critically. Encourage them to identify key issues, examine cause-effect relationships, and consider the implications and consequences of different decisions or actions.

6. Role-Play or Simulation: Have students role-play or engage in simulations to bring the case or scenario to life. Assign roles to different students and encourage them to consider the perspectives and motivations of the individuals involved. This approach allows for a more immersive and experiential learning experience.

7. Research and Investigation: Encourage students to conduct additional research to gather more information and evidence related to the case or scenario. This can involve exploring relevant sources, conducting interviews, or analysing real data. Research provides students with a deeper understanding and supports their analysis and decision-making.

8. Reflective Writing: Incorporate reflective writing activities where students express their thoughts, insights, and lessons learned from the case study or scenario. Encourage them to reflect on their decision-making process, consider alternative approaches, and identify personal and professional growth opportunities.

9. Real-Life Guest Speakers: Invite guest speakers who have real-world experience related to the case or scenario. These speakers can share their insights, perspectives, and practical knowledge, providing students with first-hand accounts and enriching the learning experience.

10. Connect to Current Events: Relate the case study or scenario to current events or contemporary issues. This helps students see the relevance and application of the subject matter in real-life situations and fosters critical thinking about the world around them.

11. Debrief and Discussion: Conclude the case study or scenario with a debriefing session. Facilitate a whole-class discussion where students can share their analyses, insights, and lessons learned. Summarise key takeaways and relate them back to the learning objectives.

Using case studies and real-life scenarios in teaching encourages active learning, critical thinking, and the application of knowledge and skills to authentic situations. It promotes deeper understanding, engagement, and the development of problem-solving abilities that students can transfer to real-world contexts.

Teaching effective speaking skills is crucial for helping students communicate their ideas clearly, confidently, and persuasively. Here are some strategies educators can use to teach these skills:

1.   Model Effective Speaking: Model good speaking skills by delivering clear, articulate, and engaging presentations or speeches in front of the class. Demonstrate effective use of voice projection, pace, and nonverbal communication.

2.   Organise Speeches or Presentations: Teach students how to Organise their speeches or presentations effectively. Emphasise the importance of a clear introduction, body with main points, and a strong conclusion. Encourage them to use transitions to ensure a smooth flow between ideas.

3.   Audience Analysis: Discuss the significance of understanding the audience. Teach students how to analyse their audience's needs, interests, and prior knowledge to tailor their message effectively. Encourage them to consider the appropriate tone and language to engage the specific audience.

4.   Vocal Techniques: Guide students on the effective use of voice in public speaking. Teach them techniques such as varying pitch, volume, and tone to convey emotions and emphasise key points. Encourage proper pronunciation, articulation, and the use of pauses for emphasis.

5.   Body Language and Nonverbal Communication: Explain the importance of body language in effective speaking. Teach students to maintain eye contact, use gestures purposefully, and exhibit open and confident body posture. Emphasise the impact of nonverbal cues on audience engagement and understanding.

6.   Use Visual Aids: Teach students how to effectively use visual aids, such as slides, props, or multimedia, to enhance their presentations. Guide them on creating visually appealing and informative visuals that support and reinforce their key messages.

7.   Practice and Rehearsal: Provide ample opportunities for students to practice their speaking skills. Encourage them to rehearse their speeches or presentations to build confidence and refine their delivery. Offer constructive feedback and suggestions for improvement during practice sessions.

8.   Impromptu Speaking: Incorporate activities that require students to think on their feet and deliver impromptu speeches. Provide prompts or discussion topics that students can respond to spontaneously. This practice helps build adaptability, critical thinking, and fluency in expressing ideas.

9.   Active Listening and Feedback: Teach students active listening skills, including how to provide constructive feedback to their peers. Encourage them to offer specific, positive feedback and suggestions for improvement. Engaging in thoughtful feedback builds a supportive speaking community.

10.   Authentic Speaking Opportunities: Create authentic speaking opportunities beyond the classroom, such as debates, panel discussions, or presentations to a wider audience. Encourage participation in public speaking events or competitions to showcase students' skills and build confidence.

11.   Reflection and Self-Assessment: Incorporate opportunities for students to reflect on their speaking performances. Encourage self-assessment, where students evaluate their own strengths, areas for improvement, and strategies they can employ in future speaking engagements.

12.   Create a Supportive Environment: Foster a positive and supportive classroom environment where students feel comfortable taking risks and expressing themselves. Encourage respect, active listening, and constructive feedback among peers. Build students' confidence by acknowledging their progress and celebrating their speaking achievements.

By incorporating these strategies, educators can help students develop effective speaking skills. These skills are valuable not only in academic settings but also in various personal and professional contexts. Developing strong speaking skills empowers students to express themselves with confidence, connect with others, and effectively convey their ideas to diverse audiences.

Mnemonic devices and memory techniques

Mnemonic devices and memory techniques can be effective tools for improving memory and enhancing learning. Here are some strategies educators can use to teach students how to utilise mnemonic devices and memory techniques:

1. Acronyms and Acrostics: Teach students to create acronyms or acrostics to remember lists or sequences of information. By forming a word or phrase using the first letter of each item, students can recall the information more easily. Encourage them to create meaningful and memorable acronyms or acrostics related to the content being studied.

2. Visualisation and Mental Imagery: Guide students to visualise vivid mental images that help them associate information with visual cues. Encourage them to create mental pictures or scenes that connect concepts or facts. The more vivid and unusual the image, the better it tends to be remembered.

3. Rhymes and Songs: Help students create rhymes, songs, or jingles to remember key information. The rhythm, rhyme, and melody can aid in encoding and recalling the material. Encourage students to use rhythm and musical patterns to structure their rhymes or songs for optimal memorisation.

4. Chunking and Grouping: Teach students to chunk or group information together to make it more manageable and memorable. Breaking down large amounts of information into smaller, Organised chunks allows for easier recall. Help students identify patterns, relationships, or categories to group related information together.

5. Method of Loci (Memory Palace): Introduce the method of loci, where students mentally associate information with specific locations or rooms in a familiar place, such as their house. As they mentally navigate through the space, they can recall the information associated with each location.

6. Mind Maps and Concept Mapping: Teach students to create visual diagrams, such as mind maps or concept maps, to Organise and connect related ideas. Encourage the use of keywords, colours, and visual elements to represent key concepts and their relationships.

7. Repetition and Spaced Practice: Emphasise the importance of repetition and spaced practice for memory retention. Encourage students to review and practice the material regularly over time, spacing out their study sessions rather than cramming. This helps consolidate memory and promotes long-term retention.

8. Self-Generated Examples and Analogies: Guide students to create their own examples and analogies to relate new information to existing knowledge or personal experiences. Encouraging students to generate their own connections and associations deepens understanding and enhances memory retrieval.

9.   Multisensory Learning: Incorporate multisensory activities to engage multiple senses, such as tactile, auditory, and visual. Encourage students to interact with materials, use manipulatives, draw diagrams, or engage in kinaesthetic activities. The more senses involved in the learning process, the stronger the memory connections tend to be.

10.   Contextualisation and Meaningful Connections: Help students make meaningful connections between new information and existing knowledge or experiences. Encourage them to relate the content to real-life scenarios, personal anecdotes, or relevant examples. When students can see the relevance and significance of the information, it becomes easier to remember.

11.   Reflection and Metacognition: Incorporate opportunities for students to reflect on their learning and memory strategies. Encourage metacognitive awareness by having students evaluate the effectiveness of different mnemonic devices and memory techniques for their own learning style. Foster self-regulated learners who can adapt their strategies based on their individual needs.

By teaching mnemonic devices and memory techniques, educators can provide students with effective tools to enhance memory, retention, and recall. These techniques not only support academic success but also promote lifelong learning and the development of effective study habits.

Integrating interdisciplinary connections in teaching allows students to explore connections and relationships between different subject areas, fostering a deeper understanding of the interconnectedness of knowledge. Here are some strategies educators can use to integrate interdisciplinary connections:

1. Identify Overlapping Concepts: Identify common concepts, themes, or issues that span multiple subject areas. Look for connections between topics in different subjects and explore how they relate to one another. For example, literature can be connected to history, science can be connected to mathematics, and art can be connected to social studies.

2. Collaborative Planning: Collaborate with colleagues from different subject areas to plan interdisciplinary units or projects. Work together to align objectives, content, and assessments across subjects. Design activities that integrate knowledge and skills from multiple disciplines and promote cross-disciplinary understanding.

3. Project-Based Learning: Implement project-based learning experiences that require students to apply knowledge and skills from different subjects to solve real-world problems or complete complex tasks. Provide opportunities for students to engage in research, analysis, synthesis, and presentation of interdisciplinary projects.

4. Cross-Curricular Units: Design cross-curricular units where students explore a central theme or question from multiple angles. Blend lessons and activities from different subjects, allowing students to make connections between disciplines. Provide opportunities for students to transfer knowledge and skills across subject areas.

5. Guest Speakers and Field Trips: Invite guest speakers from various fields or Organise field trips that relate to the interdisciplinary connections being explored. These experiences expose students to professionals who work at the intersection of different disciplines and provide real-world examples of interdisciplinary applications.

6. Integrated Assessments: Develop assessments that require students to demonstrate understanding and application of knowledge across multiple subjects. Assessments could include projects, presentations, portfolios, or performances that showcase interdisciplinary connections and depth of understanding.

7. Literature Connections: Use literature as a tool to explore interdisciplinary connections. Select books or texts that integrate multiple subjects or perspectives. Discuss the connections between the literary work and related topics in science, history, social issues, or art.

8. Technology Integration: Utilise technology tools and resources that facilitate interdisciplinary connections. Encourage students to use digital platforms for

collaborative projects, research, data analysis, or multimedia presentations. Online resources can provide interdisciplinary content, simulations, or interactive learning experiences.

9.   Reflective Discussions: Foster reflective discussions where students explore the interdisciplinary connections they have discovered. Encourage students to articulate the value and relevance of interdisciplinary learning and how it enhances their understanding of complex issues.

10.   Professional Development: Engage in professional development opportunities to enhance your own understanding of interdisciplinary connections. Attend workshops, conferences, or webinars that focus on interdisciplinary teaching strategies. Collaborate with colleagues to share ideas, resources, and best practices.

By integrating interdisciplinary connections, educators can provide students with a holistic view of knowledge and promote critical thinking, creativity, and problem-solving skills. Interdisciplinary learning prepares students to navigate the complexities of the real world by understanding how different disciplines intersect and influence one another

Encouraging metacognitive awareness

Encouraging metacognitive awareness in students is crucial for developing their ability to reflect on and regulate their own learning processes. Here are some strategies educators can use to foster metacognitive awareness:

1. Explicitly Teach Metacognitive Strategies: Introduce students to metacognitive strategies and explain their importance in learning. Teach techniques such as setting goals, monitoring progress, using self-questioning, and evaluating their own understanding. Provide explicit instruction on how to apply these strategies across different tasks and subject areas.

2. Model Metacognitive Thinking: Model metacognitive thinking by verbalising your own thought processes during lessons or problem-solving activities. Share your thinking strategies, decision-making processes, and how you self-assess and adjust your learning. Demonstrate the value of metacognitive reflection and decision-making in your own practice.

3. Reflective Journals or Learning Logs: Incorporate regular opportunities for students to engage in reflective writing. Encourage them to keep a journal or learning log where they can reflect on their learning experiences, challenges faced, strategies employed, and lessons learned. Provide prompts or guiding questions to stimulate metacognitive thinking.

4. Classroom Discussions: Facilitate classroom discussions that promote metacognitive awareness. Ask students to reflect on their learning processes, discuss their approaches to problem-solving, or share strategies that have worked for them. Encourage students to share their metacognitive insights with their peers and learn from one another.

5. Self-Questioning: Teach students to ask themselves questions that promote metacognitive thinking. Encourage them to ask questions such as "What do I already know about this topic?" or "How well do I understand this concept?" These questions prompt students to reflect on their prior knowledge, monitor their understanding, and identify areas for further learning.

6. Goal Setting: Guide students in setting specific, achievable learning goals. Teach them how to break larger goals into smaller, manageable steps. Encourage students to reflect on their progress toward their goals and adjust their strategies accordingly.

7. Think-Alouds: Incorporate think-aloud activities where students verbalise their thinking processes while completing a task or solving a problem. This allows students to articulate their thoughts, make their thinking visible, and gain insight into their own cognitive processes.

8. Scaffolded Support: Provide scaffolds and support to help students develop metacognitive skills. This could include graphic Organisers, checklists, or templates that guide students in setting goals, monitoring progress, and evaluating their learning. Gradually release responsibility as students become more proficient in metacognitive thinking.

9. Peer Feedback and Collaboration: Encourage peer feedback and collaboration that focuses on metacognitive aspects of learning. Encourage students to provide feedback on each other's strategies, processes, and reflections. Peer discussions can help students gain new perspectives and insights into their own learning approaches.

10. Reflection on Assessments: After assessments, guide students in reflecting on their performance and learning outcomes. Help them identify strengths and areas for improvement, and develop strategies to address weaknesses. Encourage students to see assessments as opportunities for growth and learning rather than simply as a grade.

By fostering metacognitive awareness, educators empower students to become more independent and self-regulated learners. Developing metacognitive skills helps students understand their own thinking processes, make deliberate learning choices, and adapt their strategies for improved learning outcomes. Metacognitive awareness prepares students to be lifelong learners who can take ownership of their learning and continuously improve their learning strategies.

Educators Teaching Skills

Student Assessment:

Please complete all questions and projects

Module 1: Communication in the Training Centre/ Classroom

These assessment questions and sample answers provide insights into how educators communicate effectively in the training classroom. The answers should reflect the educators' ability to engage learners, adapt their communication style, and create a positive and inclusive learning environment

Below are assessment questions along with sample answers to evaluate educators' ability to communicate effectively in the training classroom:

1. Question: How do you ensure that your training materials and instructions are clear and easy to understand for all participants?

2. Question: How do you handle questions and feedback from participants during training sessions?

3. Question: Explain your approach to providing constructive feedback to participants without discouraging their engagement or confidence.

4. Question: How do you encourage active participation and interaction among learners during training sessions?

5. Question: How do you use visual aids, such as slides or handouts, to enhance communication and understanding during training?

6. Question: Describe a challenging situation where you needed to de-escalate tensions or conflicts among participants using effective communication techniques.

7.   Question: How do you adjust your communication pace and tone to match the needs and comfort level of your audience?

8.   Question: How do you use storytelling or real-life examples to make complex concepts more relatable and understandable for participants?

9.   Question: How do you assess participants' comprehension and progress throughout the training, and how do you adjust your communication accordingly?

10.   Question: Describe how you use ice-breakers or team-building activities to establish rapport and trust among learners at the beginning of a training session.

Module 2: Effective Verbal and Non-Verbal Communication

These assessment questions and sample answers provide insights into how educators effectively use both verbal and non-verbal communication in the training classroom. The answers should reflect the educators' ability to engage learners, adapt communication styles, and create a positive and inclusive learning environment through their words and non-verbal cues.

Below are assessment questions along with sample answers to evaluate educators' effective verbal and non-verbal communication in the training classroom:

1. Question: How do you ensure your verbal communication is clear and easily understood by participants?

2. Question: Describe how you maintain an engaging and energetic tone during your training sessions.

3. Question: How do you use body language to convey enthusiasm and engagement during your training?

4. Question: Explain how you adapt your verbal communication style to suit different learning preferences among participants.

5. Question: How do you handle challenging or difficult questions from participants while maintaining a positive and respectful atmosphere?

6. Question: Describe how you use non-verbal cues, such as facial expressions and gestures, to reinforce key messages during your training.

7. Question: How do you use pauses strategically in your verbal communication to allow participants time to process information?

8. Question: Explain how you encourage active participation through your verbal communication.

9. Question: How do you use verbal cues, such as verbal affirmations or encouragement, to create a positive learning environment?

10. Question: How do you adjust your speaking pace to ensure clarity and understanding for all participants?

Module 3: Structures of Participation

These assessment questions and sample answers provide insights into how educators structure participation in the training classroom. The answers should reflect the educators' ability to promote active participation, accommodate diverse learning preferences, and create an inclusive and collaborative learning environment

Below are assessment questions along with sample answers to evaluate educators' structures of participation in the training classroom:

1. Question: How do you encourage active participation from all participants during training sessions?

2. Question: Describe a specific activity you use to promote engagement and participation among reluctant learners.

3. Question: How do you ensure that quieter participants have an equal chance to contribute and be heard during training?

4. Question: How do you handle dominating participants to ensure that others have a chance to participate as well?

5. Question: How do you promote a collaborative learning environment that values the perspectives and contributions of all participants?

6. Question: Describe a technique you use to encourage participants to ask questions and seek clarification during the training.

7. Question: How do you adapt your structures of participation to accommodate different learning preferences and personalities among participants?

8. Question: Explain how you handle disagreements or conflicting opinions among participants while maintaining a respectful learning environment.

9. Question: How do you use technology or online platforms to enhance participation and engagement in virtual training sessions?

10. Question: Describe a technique you use to assess participants' understanding and retention of the training material during and after the session.

ISBN: 9798872216605   A.M. McIlwraith. FAIBHS., D.S.Ch.   Page 147

Module 4: Using Classroom Talk to Stimulate Students' Thinking

These assessment questions and sample answers provide insights into how educators use classroom talk effectively to stimulate students' thinking and promote active participation in the training classroom. The answers should reflect the educators' ability to ask thought-provoking questions, create a supportive learning environment, and encourage collaborative thinking among students.

Below are assessment questions along with sample answers to evaluate educators' ability to use classroom talk effectively to stimulate students' thinking in the training classroom:

1. Question: How do you use open-ended questions to encourage critical thinking and active participation among students?

2. Question: Describe a specific scenario where you used follow-up questions to delve deeper into a student's response and expand their thinking.

3. Question: How do you encourage students to build upon each other's ideas and engage in collaborative thinking?

4. Question: Explain how you use wait time to allow students the opportunity to process questions and formulate thoughtful responses.

5. Question: How do you use probing questions to challenge students' assumptions and encourage critical analysis?

6.   Question: Describe a technique you use to create a safe and supportive environment for students to express their opinions and share ideas openly.

7.   Question: How do you use classroom talk to connect new concepts with students' prior knowledge and experiences?

8.   Question: Explain how you facilitate student-led discussions to encourage ownership of learning and self-directed thinking.

9.   Question: How do you use positive reinforcement and affirmations to validate students' contributions during classroom discussions?

10.   Question: Describe a strategy you use to draw connections between different ideas shared by students to foster deeper understanding.

Module 5: Diploma Educators "Teaching Skills" - First Assessment
Project: To Be Assigned

Module 6: Selecting General Learning Goals

These assessment questions and sample answers provide insights into how educators select general learning goals in the classroom. The answers should reflect the educators' ability to align goals with the curriculum, differentiate for diverse learners, involve students in the goal-setting process, and use goals to guide instruction and assessment effectively.

Below are assessment questions along with sample answers to evaluate educators' ability to select general learning goals in the classroom:

1. Question: How do you determine the general learning goals for your classroom curriculum?

2. Question: Describe a process you use to prioritize and select the most relevant general learning goals for your students.

3. Question: How do you ensure that the selected general learning goals align with the overall educational objectives of the school or district?

4. Question: How do you differentiate general learning goals for students with varying abilities and learning styles in your classroom?

5. Question: Explain how you communicate the general learning goals to students and involve them in the goal-setting process.

6. Question: How do you ensure that general learning goals are specific, measurable, achievable, relevant, and time-bound (SMART)?

7. Question: Describe a situation where you had to revise or modify general learning goals based on students' progress and needs.

8. Question: How do you incorporate interdisciplinary connections when selecting general learning goals?

9. Question: Explain how you use general learning goals to guide your lesson planning and instructional strategies.

10. Question: How do you assess students' progress towards the general learning goals and adjust your instructional approach accordingly?

Module 7: Formulating Educational Objectives

These assessment questions and sample answers provide insights into how educators formulate educational objectives in the classroom. The answers should reflect the educators' ability to create clear, aligned, and measurable objectives, as well as their skill in differentiating and revising objectives based on ongoing assessment data and students' needs.

Below are assessment questions along with sample answers to evaluate educators' ability to formulate educational objectives in the classroom:

1.   Question: How do you formulate clear and specific educational objectives for your lessons or units?

2.   Question: Describe a process you use to align educational objectives with the overall curriculum and learning standards.

3.   Question: How do you differentiate educational objectives to accommodate students with varying abilities and learning needs?

4.   Question: Explain how you communicate educational objectives to students and involve them in the learning process.

5.   Question: How do you prioritize educational objectives to focus on the most critical concepts and skills for student learning?

6.   Question: Describe how you align educational objectives with assessment strategies to measure students' progress effectively.

7.   Question: How do you adapt and revise educational objectives when needed based on ongoing student assessment data?

8.   Question: Explain how you integrate 21st-century skills, such as critical thinking, creativity, and collaboration, into your educational objectives.

9.   Question: Describe a situation where you used backward design to formulate educational objectives for a specific unit or project.

10.   Question: How do you use educational objectives to guide your lesson planning and instructional strategies?

Module 8: Students as a Source of Instructional Goals

These assessment questions and sample answers provide insights into how educators use instructional goals in the classroom. The answers should reflect the educators' ability to set clear and aligned goals, differentiate instruction, involve students in the learning process, and use goals to drive effective lesson planning and assessment

Below are assessment questions along with sample answers to evaluate educators' use of instructional goals in the classroom:

1.   Question: How do you set clear and specific instructional goals for your lessons or units?

2.   Question: Describe how you align instructional goals with the overall curriculum and learning standards.

3.   Question: How do you differentiate instructional goals to meet the diverse learning needs and abilities of your students?

4.   Question: Explain how you communicate instructional goals to students and involve them in the learning process.

5.   Question: How do you prioritise instructional goals to focus on the most essential content and skills for student learning?

6.   Question: Describe how you align instructional goals with assessment strategies to measure students' progress effectively.

7.   Question: How do you adjust instructional goals based on ongoing student assessment data and their progress?

8.   Question: Explain how you incorporate real-life applications and relevance into instructional goals to enhance student engagement.

.

9.   Question: Describe a situation where you used backward design to develop instructional goals for a specific unit or project.

10. Question: How do you use instructional goals to guide your lesson planning and ensure a coherent and purposeful learning experience?

Module 9: Enhancing Student Learning

These assessment questions and sample answers provide insights into how educators enhance student learning in the classroom. The answers should reflect the educators' ability to create a positive and inclusive learning environment, use formative assessments to guide instruction, differentiate instruction, and promote active learning, critical thinking, and student autonomy

Below are assessment questions along with sample answers to evaluate educators' ability to enhance student learning in the classroom:

1. Question: How do you create a positive and inclusive learning environment that fosters student engagement and motivation?

2. Question: Describe a situation where you used formative assessments to monitor student progress and adjust your teaching accordingly.

3. Question: How do you differentiate instruction to meet the diverse learning needs and abilities of your students?

4. Question: Explain how you incorporate real-world connections and examples into your lessons to make learning relevant and meaningful for students.

5. Question: How do you encourage active learning and critical thinking in the classroom?

6. Question: Describe how you provide timely and constructive feedback to students to support their learning and growth.

7.   Question: How do you promote a growth mind-set in your classroom to inspire students to embrace challenges and view failures as opportunities for learning?

8.   Question: Explain how you integrate technology and digital resources to enhance student learning experiences.

9.   Question: Describe a strategy you use to foster a sense of ownership and autonomy in students' learning journeys.

10.   Question: How do you promote collaboration and peer learning among students to enhance their overall learning experience?

Module 10: Creating Bridges between Goals and Experiences

These assessment questions and sample answers provide insights into how educators create bridges between learning goals and students' experiences in the classroom. The answers should reflect the educators' ability to connect learning objectives to real-life experiences, scaffold learning, promote student autonomy, and use formative assessments to track progress and adjust instruction accordingly.

Below are assessment questions along with sample answers to evaluate educators' ability to create bridges between goals and experiences in the classroom:

1. Question: How do you connect the learning goals and objectives to real-life experiences and prior knowledge of students?

2. Question: Describe a specific lesson where you used experiential learning to bridge the gap between learning goals and students' experiences.

3. Question: How do you ensure that students understand the purpose and relevance of the learning goals in relation to their future academic and personal growth?

4. Question: Explain how you scaffold learning experiences to support students in reaching their learning goals step-by-step.

5. Question: How do you incorporate interdisciplinary connections to create bridges between different subjects and learning goals?

6. Question: Describe a strategy you use to encourage students to set personal learning goals that align with the broader learning objectives.

7. Question: How do you promote self-directed learning and independent thinking to bridge the gap between goals and students' own experiences?

8. Question: Explain how you use formative assessments to track students' progress and adjust learning experiences to better align with their needs.

9. Question: Describe a specific activity where you used technology to bridge the gap between learning goals and students' experiences.

10. Question: How do you encourage students to reflect on their learning experiences and make connections between their achievements and the broader learning goals?

Module 12: Behaviour and Goals as Motivation Sources

These assessment questions and sample answers provide insights into how educators use behaviour and goals as motivation sources in the classroom. The answers should reflect the educators' ability to implement positive reinforcement, goal setting, intrinsic motivation techniques, behaviour management, and progress monitoring to create a supportive and motivating learning environment.

1. Question: How do you use positive reinforcement and rewards to motivate students towards achieving their learning goals?

2. Question: Describe a situation where you effectively used goal setting to motivate students to excel in their academic performance.

3. Question: How do you create a supportive classroom culture that encourages students to take ownership of their learning and set personal growth goals?

4. Question: Explain how you use behaviour management strategies to address challenging behaviours and maintain a positive learning environment.

5. Question: Describe a specific technique you use to promote intrinsic motivation among students.

6.   Question: How do you provide opportunities for students to reflect on their progress and celebrate their achievements?

7.   Question: How do you use goal progress monitoring to track students' development and offer guidance to those who may be struggling?

8.   Question: Describe a strategy you use to help students see the connection between their efforts and their academic achievements.

9.   Question: How do you encourage students to set both short-term and long-term goals to sustain their motivation throughout the academic year?

10.   Question: Explain how you promote a growth mind-set in your classroom to inspire students to embrace challenges and persevere in their learning.

Module 13: Motivation Related to Attributions and Interests

These assessment questions and sample answers provide insights into how educators address motivation related to attributions and interests in the classroom. The answers should reflect the educators' ability to foster a growth mind-set, leverage students' interests, provide choices and challenges, offer meaningful feedback, and create a supportive learning environment that promotes intrinsic motivation

Below are assessment questions along with sample answers to evaluate educators' ability to understand and address motivation related to attributions and interests in the classroom:

1. Question: How do you foster a growth mind-set among your students to encourage them to see challenges as opportunities for learning and growth?

2. Question: Describe a situation where you helped a student overcome a negative attribution or self-perception about their academic abilities.

3. Question: How do you leverage students' interests and passions to enhance their motivation and engagement in the learning process?

4. Question: Explain how you provide choices and autonomy in learning activities to increase students' intrinsic motivation.

5. Question: Describe a strategy you use to help students set meaningful learning goals that are connected to their interests and aspirations.

6. Question: How do you use positive feedback and recognition to reinforce students' efforts and accomplishments in the classroom?

7. Question: Explain how you provide challenges and opportunities for success to cater to the varying levels of student ability and interests.

8. Question: Describe a situation where you helped a student develop a sense of competence and self-efficacy in a subject they initially found challenging.

9. Question: How do you create a positive and supportive classroom culture where students feel comfortable taking academic risks and trying new approaches to learning?

10. Question: Explain how you address students' individual interests within the constraints of the curriculum to keep them engaged and motivated.

Module 14: Self Efficacy

These assessment questions and sample answers provide insights into how educators support self-efficacy in the classroom. The answers should reflect the educators' ability to promote self-belief, use goal setting and feedback to support personal growth, create a supportive learning environment, and foster a growth mind-set that emphasizes effort and resilience.

Below are assessment questions along with sample answers to evaluate educators' ability to understand and support self-efficacy in the classroom:

1. Question: How do you promote a sense of self-efficacy among your students to believe in their ability to succeed academically?

2. Question: Describe a situation where you helped a student develop a stronger sense of self-efficacy in a subject they previously found challenging.

3. Question: How do you use goal setting and individualized learning plans to support students' self-efficacy and personal growth?

4. Question: Explain how you use positive affirmations and constructive feedback to nurture students' self-belief and confidence.

5. Question: Describe a strategy you use to help students overcome self-doubt and fear of failure.

6. Question: How do you create a supportive classroom environment where students feel comfortable taking academic risks and trying new approaches to learning?

7. Question: Explain how you use differentiation and flexible grouping to address individual learning needs and build students' confidence.

8. Question: Describe a situation where you helped a student overcome academic setbacks and maintain a positive outlook on their abilities.

9. Question: How do you foster a growth mind-set and emphasize the role of effort and perseverance in achieving success?

10. Question: Explain how you celebrate students' achievements and growth to reinforce their self-efficacy and boost their confidence.

Module 15: Self-Determination

These assessment questions and sample answers provide insights into how educators support self-determination in the classroom. The answers should reflect the educators' ability to encourage student autonomy, support goal-setting and self-reflection, foster a positive classroom culture, provide relevant learning experiences, and recognize and celebrate students' strengths and talents to enhance their self-determination.

Below are assessment questions along with sample answers to evaluate educators' ability to understand and support self-determination in the classroom:

1. Question: How do you encourage student autonomy and choice in the learning process to foster self-determination?

2. Question: Describe a situation where you helped a student develop a stronger sense of self-determination and ownership over their learning.

3. Question: How do you support students in setting and working towards self-determined goals that align with their interests and aspirations?

4. Question: Explain how you use self-reflection and goal-setting activities to develop students' self-awareness and enhance their self-determination.

5. Question: Describe a strategy you use to help students overcome obstacles and develop a sense of agency in their academic pursuits.

6.   Question: How do you foster a classroom culture that values and celebrates individual student contributions and voices?

7.   Question: Explain how you use authentic and relevant learning experiences to promote students' intrinsic motivation and self-determination.

8.   Question: Describe a situation where you used collaborative learning activities to foster a sense of empowerment and collective responsibility among students.

9.   Question: How do you provide opportunities for students to develop and showcase their talents and strengths, fostering self-determination in their learning journey?

10.   Question: Explain how you adapt your teaching approach to accommodate students' interests and learning preferences, promoting their sense of autonomy and self-determination.

Module 16: Combining Motivation Theories

These assessment questions and sample answers provide insights into how educators effectively combine motivation theories in the classroom. The answers should reflect the educators' ability to design engaging and motivating learning experiences, leverage a variety of motivational theories, and foster a positive and supportive learning environment that addresses students' needs and aspirations

Below are assessment questions along with sample answers to evaluate educators' ability to effectively combine motivation theories in the classroom:

1. Question: How do you incorporate aspects of both intrinsic and extrinsic motivation in your teaching to engage and inspire students?

2. Question: Describe a lesson where you used self-determination theory to empower students to take ownership of their learning.

3. Question: How do you incorporate elements of both goal-setting theory and expectancy theory to enhance students' motivation and performance?

4. Question: Explain how you utilize positive reinforcement from behaviourism and cognitive evaluation theory to create a positive and motivating classroom atmosphere.

5. Question: Describe a strategy you use to leverage elements of the hierarchy of needs theory and self-determination theory to meet students' psychological and emotional needs.

6. Question: How do you integrate elements of the cognitive theory of motivation and the attribution theory to help students develop a positive outlook on their abilities and effort?

7. Question: Explain how you use elements of both the expectancy-value theory and the equity theory to maintain a fair and motivating classroom atmosphere.

8. Question: Describe a lesson where you integrated elements of the self-efficacy theory and the achievement goal theory to boost students' confidence and willingness to tackle challenging tasks.

9. Question: How do you balance between intrinsic interest and extrinsic rewards when designing learning experiences to maintain students' long-term motivation?

10. Question: Explain how you use elements of reinforcement theory and goal-setting theory to create a positive feedback loop that reinforces students' progress and effort.

Module 17: Diploma Educators "Teaching Skills" - Third Assessment
Project : Prepare a detailed business plan

Educators Teaching Skills

Student Assessment:

Educators Copy

Questions are completed by student.
Answers provide foundation and example scenarios.
Projects should be assigned based on industry specific
requirements

Module 1: Communication in the Training Centre/ Classroom

These assessment questions and sample answers provide insights into how educators communicate effectively in the training classroom. The answers should reflect the educators' ability to engage learners, adapt their communication style, and create a positive and inclusive learning environment

Below are assessment questions along with sample answers to evaluate educators' ability to communicate effectively in the training classroom:

11. Question: How do you ensure that your training materials and instructions are clear and easy to understand for all participants?

    Answer: Use simple and concise language in training materials and instructions. also avoid jargon and technical terms whenever possible. Additionally, encourage participants to ask questions and seek clarification if they don't understand something.

12. Question: How do you handle questions and feedback from participants during training sessions?

    Answer: welcome questions and feedback from participants throughout the session. When someone asks a question, listen carefully, and if the educator doesn't have an immediate answer, promise to follow up with them later. Make sure to create a safe and non-judgmental environment where participants feel comfortable sharing their thoughts.

13. Question: Explain your approach to providing constructive feedback to participants without discouraging their engagement or confidence.

    Answer: When providing feedback, always start with positive reinforcement, acknowledging what the participant did well. Then, gently offer suggestions for improvement, focusing on specific behaviours or areas for growth. Make sure to emphasize that feedback is meant to help them improve and that mistakes are a natural part of the learning process.

14. Question: How do you encourage active participation and interaction among learners during training sessions?

    Answer: use various interactive techniques, such as group discussions, role-playing, and hands-on activities, to engage participants actively. Encourage everyone to contribute their ideas and perspectives, and create opportunities for collaborative learning experiences.

15. Question: How do you use visual aids, such as slides or handouts, to enhance communication and understanding during training?

Answer: use visual aids to complement verbal communication and make complex concepts more accessible. Ensure that the visuals are clearing, well-organized, and support the main points being discussed. Visual aids help reinforce key information and keep participants engaged.

16. Question: Describe a challenging situation where you needed to de-escalate tensions or conflicts among participants using effective communication techniques.

    Answer: the educator outlines an example of a disagreement between two participants. Outline key intervention skills egg; actively listening to both sides and validating their perspectives. Encouragement to find common ground and build on each other's ideas, fostering a collaborative problem-solving approach.

17. Question: How do you adjust your communication pace and tone to match the needs and comfort level of your audience?

    Answer: pay close attention to participants' responses and body language during the training. If there are signs of confusion or disengagement, slow down the pace and offer additional explanations. On the other hand, if the audience is responsive and engaged, maintain a lively and enthusiastic tone to keep the energy high.

18. Question: How do you use storytelling or real-life examples to make complex concepts more relatable and understandable for participants?

    Answer: Storytelling and real-life examples are powerful tools to make abstract concepts more concrete and relevant. Share anecdotes or case studies that illustrate how the concepts apply in real-world situations. This helps participants connect the theoretical knowledge to practical applications.

19. Question: How do you assess participants' comprehension and progress throughout the training, and how do you adjust your communication accordingly?

    Answer: use regular quizzes, polls, and group discussions to gauge participants' understanding and progress. Based on their responses identify areas that may need further clarification or reinforcement. Adapt communication style and re-explain concepts if needed, ensuring everyone stays on the same page.

20. Question: Describe how you use ice-breakers or team-building activities to establish rapport and trust among learners at the beginning of a training session.

Answer: At the beginning of a training session, use ice-breakers or team-building activities to create a relaxed and welcoming atmosphere. These activities help participants get to know each other, build trust, and create a supportive learning environment. As a result, participants feel more comfortable sharing their thoughts and ideas throughout the training.

Module 2: Effective Verbal and Non-Verbal Communication

These assessment questions and sample answers provide insights into how educators effectively use both verbal and non-verbal communication in the training classroom. The answers should reflect the educators' ability to engage learners, adapt communication styles, and create a positive and inclusive learning environment through their words and non-verbal cues.

Below are assessment questions along with sample answers to evaluate educators' effective verbal and non-verbal communication in the training classroom:

11. Question: How do you ensure your verbal communication is clear and easily understood by participants?

    Answer: use straightforward language and avoid using technical jargon or complex terms whenever possible. Also check for participants' understanding by encouraging questions and summarizing key points throughout the training.

12. Question: Describe how you maintain an engaging and energetic tone during your training sessions.

    Answer: vary the tone and pitch of the voice to keep the participants engaged. By using a conversational and enthusiastic tone, aim to capture their attention and maintain their interest throughout the session.

13. Question: How do you use body language to convey enthusiasm and engagement during your training?

    Answer: use open body language, make eye contact with participants, and smile to show the educator is approachable and enthusiastic about the topic. also use gestures and movement to emphasize key points and maintain the audience's focus.

14. Question: Explain how you adapt your verbal communication style to suit different learning preferences among participants.

    Answer: recognize that participants have diverse learning preferences, use a mix of auditory, visual, and kinaesthetic techniques. This includes explaining concepts verbally, using visual aids, and incorporating hands-on activities to cater to different learning styles.

15. Question: How do you handle challenging or difficult questions from participants while maintaining a positive and respectful atmosphere?

Answer: When faced with challenging questions, respond with patience and respect. If the educator doesn't have an immediate answer, acknowledge the question and promise to follow up after researching or consulting relevant sources.

16. Question: Describe how you use non-verbal cues, such as facial expressions and gestures, to reinforce key messages during your training.

Answer: Non-verbal cues play a vital role in reinforcing key messages. Use facial expressions to show excitement, surprise, or concern, depending on the context. Additionally, use gestures to emphasize important points and create a visual connection with the participants.

17. Question: How do you use pauses strategically in your verbal communication to allow participants time to process information?

Answer: incorporate intentional pauses during the training to give participants time to absorb the information presented. Pauses allow students to reflect on the content and ask questions if needed, promoting a more thoughtful learning experience.

18. Question: Explain how you encourage active participation through your verbal communication.

Answer: encourage active participation by asking open-ended questions, seeking input from participants, and inviting them to share their experiences and insights. By creating a participatory environment, it will foster engagement and facilitate a collaborative learning process.

19. Question: How do you use verbal cues, such as verbal affirmations or encouragement, to create a positive learning environment?

Answer: Verbal cues like affirmations, encouragement, and positive reinforcement are essential in creating a supportive atmosphere. Use phrases like "Great job!" or "Well done!" to acknowledge participants' contributions and efforts, promoting confidence and motivation.

20. Question: How do you adjust your speaking pace to ensure clarity and understanding for all participants?

Answer: pay attention to participants' reactions and adjust my speaking pace accordingly. If you notice confusion or disengagement, slow down to allow more time for comprehension. On the other hand, if participants are actively engaged, maintain an appropriate pace to keep the momentum going.

Module 3: Structures of Participation

These assessment questions and sample answers provide insights into how educators structure participation in the training classroom. The answers should reflect the educators' ability to promote active participation, accommodate diverse learning preferences, and create an inclusive and collaborative learning environment

Below are assessment questions along with sample answers to evaluate educators' structures of participation in the training classroom:

11. Question: How do you encourage active participation from all participants during training sessions?

      Answer: employ various strategies to encourage active participation. This includes asking open-ended questions, creating small group discussions, using interactive activities, and providing opportunities for participants to share their experiences and insights.

12. Question: Describe a specific activity you use to promote engagement and participation among reluctant learners.

      Answer: One effective activity is the "Think-Pair-Share" technique. Ask thought-provoking questions, give participants a moment to think individually, and then have them pair up to discuss their thoughts before sharing their ideas with the larger group. This approach encourages participation and fosters collaboration.

13. Question: How do you ensure that quieter participants have an equal chance to contribute and be heard during training?

      Answer: To ensure everyone's voice is heard, make a conscious effort to call on quieter participants and create a safe space for them to share their thoughts. Use techniques like "round-robin" discussions to give each participant an opportunity to contribute without feeling pressured.

14. Question: How do you handle dominating participants to ensure that others have a chance to participate as well?

      Answer: When dealing with dominating participants, gently intervene by thanking them for their input and then redirecting the discussion to encourage input from others. You might say, "Thank you for sharing. Now, let's hear from others who haven't had a chance to contribute yet."

15. Question: How do you promote a collaborative learning environment that values the perspectives and contributions of all participants?

Answer: set the tone for a collaborative environment by modelling respectful and inclusive behaviour. Emphasize the importance of diverse perspectives and create opportunities for participants to work together, share ideas, and build on each other's contributions.

16.   Question: Describe a technique you use to encourage participants to ask questions and seek clarification during the training.

Answer: establish an open-door policy for questions and actively encourage participants to ask whenever they need clarification. You might say, "Please don't hesitate to ask questions at any time. Your curiosity and engagement are essential to the learning process."

17.   Question: How do you adapt your structures of participation to accommodate different learning preferences and personalities among participants?

Answer: offer a variety of participation options to cater to diverse learning preferences. For visual learners, use visual aids and handouts. Auditory learners benefit from group discussions and verbal explanations, while kinaesthetic learners engage in hands-on activities.

18.   Question: Explain how you handle disagreements or conflicting opinions among participants while maintaining a respectful learning environment.

Answer: acknowledge differing opinions and emphasize that respectful dialogue is encouraged. Encourage participants to focus on the issue at hand rather than personal attacks. If necessary, facilitate a discussion that allows participants to express their viewpoints while maintaining a positive atmosphere.

19.   Question: How do you use technology or online platforms to enhance participation and engagement in virtual training sessions?

Answer: In virtual training, use tools like polling, chat features, breakout rooms, and interactive quizzes to foster participation and engagement. These technologies create opportunities for participants to actively contribute and interact with the content.

20.   Question: Describe a technique you use to assess participants' understanding and retention of the training material during and after the session.

Answer: Throughout the training, use quick quizzes or polls to gauge participants' understanding. Additionally, allocate time for reflection and ask participants to summarize key takeaways at the end of the session to assess their retention.

Module 4: Using Classroom Talk to Stimulate Students' Thinking

These assessment questions and sample answers provide insights into how educators use classroom talk effectively to stimulate students' thinking and promote active participation in the training classroom. The answers should reflect the educators' ability to ask thought-provoking questions, create a supportive learning environment, and encourage collaborative thinking among students.

Below are assessment questions along with sample answers to evaluate educators' ability to use classroom talk effectively to stimulate students' thinking in the training classroom:

11. Question: How do you use open-ended questions to encourage critical thinking and active participation among students?

    Answer: Open-ended questions invite students to think critically and express their ideas. use questions like "What are your thoughts on this topic?" or "How might you approach this problem differently?" to stimulate deeper thinking and engage students in meaningful discussions.

12. Question: Describe a specific scenario where you used follow-up questions to delve deeper into a student's response and expand their thinking.

    Answer: During a group discussion, a student shared an interesting perspective on a historical event. To explore their idea further, ask follow-up questions like "Can you provide more evidence to support your view?" and "What other factors might have influenced this event?" This approach encouraged the student to analyse their argument more deeply.

13. Question: How do you encourage students to build upon each other's ideas and engage in collaborative thinking?

    Answer: create a collaborative learning environment where students feel comfortable sharing their ideas and responding to each other's contributions. Ask questions like "Can anyone add to what John just said?" or "Does anyone have a different perspective on this topic?"

14. Question: Explain how you use wait time to allow students the opportunity to process questions and formulate thoughtful responses.

    Answer: use wait time to give students a chance to process questions and gather their thoughts before responding. Count to five silently after asking a question, allowing students to feel comfortable without rushing their responses.

15. Question: How do you use probing questions to challenge students' assumptions and encourage critical analysis?

    Answer: Probing questions are essential to challenge students' thinking and promote critical analysis. For example, ask, "What led you to that conclusion?" or "How might your perspective change if you considered a different viewpoint?"

16. Question: Describe a technique you use to create a safe and supportive environment for students to express their opinions and share ideas openly.

    Answer: establish classroom norms early on, emphasizing the importance of respecting diverse viewpoints and creating a safe space for open discussion. Reinforce this by providing positive feedback when students share their ideas and fostering a culture of mutual respect.

17. Question: How do you use classroom talk to connect new concepts with students' prior knowledge and experiences?

    Answer: start discussions by asking students what they already know about a topic or how it relates to their lives. By making connections with their prior knowledge and experiences, you can build a foundation for new concepts and facilitate deeper learning.

18. Question: Explain how you facilitate student-led discussions to encourage ownership of learning and self-directed thinking.

    Answer: Student-led discussions empower students to take ownership of their learning. Assign roles or guiding questions to students to facilitate discussions. This approach promotes self-directed thinking as they lead the conversation and explore topics of interest.

19. Question: How do you use positive reinforcement and affirmations to validate students' contributions during classroom discussions?

    Answer: provide positive reinforcement by acknowledging and affirming students' thoughtful responses. For example, say, "That's an excellent point,

Emma!" or "I appreciate your unique perspective, Adam." This positive feedback encourages active participation and boosts students' confidence.

20.   Question: Describe a strategy you use to draw connections between different ideas shared by students to foster deeper understanding.

   Answer: When students share diverse ideas, help them see connections by summarizing the common themes or linking ideas together. I might say, "It seems like several of you are exploring similar aspects of this topic, which shows how complex and multifaceted it is."

Module 5: Diploma Educators "Teaching Skills" - First Assessment Project:

Module 6: Selecting General Learning Goals

These assessment questions and sample answers provide insights into how educators select general learning goals in the classroom. The answers should reflect the educators' ability to align goals with the curriculum, differentiate for diverse learners, involve students in the goal-setting process, and use goals to guide instruction and assessment effectively.

Below are assessment questions along with sample answers to evaluate educators' ability to select general learning goals in the classroom:

11. Question: How do you determine the general learning goals for your classroom curriculum?

    Answer: start by reviewing the curriculum guidelines and standards set by the education board or institution. Then consider the needs, interests, and abilities of my students. Based on this information, create broad learning goals that align with the curriculum and cater to the unique characteristics of my class.

12. Question: Describe a process you use to prioritize and select the most relevant general learning goals for your students.

    Answer: prioritize learning goals based on their relevance to students' academic growth and personal development. Consider which goals will have the most significant impact on their overall learning and future success. Also seek input from colleagues and students to ensure a comprehensive perspective.

13. Question: How do you ensure that the selected general learning goals align with the overall educational objectives of the school or district?

    Answer: collaborate with other educators and administrators to align my classroom learning goals with the broader educational objectives of the school or district. Attend professional development sessions and department meetings to stay updated on the school's educational priorities and standards.

14. Question: How do you differentiate general learning goals for students with varying abilities and learning styles in your classroom?

    Answer: adapt general learning goals to meet the diverse needs of my students. Provide additional support or challenges based on individual abilities, and offer different approaches to meet various learning styles. This ensures that all students can progress towards the same overarching learning goals while taking different paths to get there.

15. Question: Explain how you communicate the general learning goals to students and involve them in the goal-setting process.

    Answer: introduce learning goals to my students at the beginning of each unit or topic. I discuss the purpose and relevance of these goals and involve students in setting individual learning objectives. By including them in the goal-setting process, I foster a sense of ownership and motivation for their learning journey.

16. Question: How do you ensure that general learning goals are specific, measurable, achievable, relevant, and time-bound (SMART)?

    Answer: ensure that each general learning goal meets the SMART criteria by clearly defining the outcome, setting measurable criteria for success, and aligning it with the students' current abilities and interests. Also establish a reasonable timeline for achieving the goals.

17. Question: Describe a situation where you had to revise or modify general learning goals based on students' progress and needs.

    Answer: During a formative assessment, take notice if some students were struggling to grasp a specific concept. To address this, revise the learning goal, breaking it down into smaller steps and providing additional support to help students achieve success.

18. Question: How do you incorporate interdisciplinary connections when selecting general learning goals?

    Answer: consider how the general learning goals can be integrated with other subject areas. By finding connections between different disciplines, create a more comprehensive and holistic learning experience for my students.

19. Question: Explain how you use general learning goals to guide your lesson planning and instructional strategies.

    Answer: General learning goals serve as a roadmap for my lesson planning. design activities, assessments, and instructional strategies that align with the learning goals to ensure that my teaching is purposeful and focused on achieving the desired outcomes.

20. Question: How do you assess students' progress towards the general learning goals and adjust your instructional approach accordingly?

    Answer: regularly assess students' progress through formative assessments, quizzes, and observations. Based on the results, identify areas where students may need additional support or challenges. Adjust instructional approach to meet their needs and ensure continued progress towards the general learning goals.

Module 7: Formulating Educational Objectives

These assessment questions and sample answers provide insights into how educators formulate educational objectives in the classroom. The answers should reflect the educators' ability to create clear, aligned, and measurable objectives, as well as their skill in differentiating and revising objectives based on ongoing assessment data and students' needs.

Below are assessment questions along with sample answers to evaluate educators' ability to formulate educational objectives in the classroom:

11. Question: How do you formulate clear and specific educational objectives for your lessons or units?

    Answer: To formulate clear and specific educational objectives, use the SMART criteria: Specific, Measurable, Achievable, Relevant, and Time-bound. I focus on what students will learn, how their progress will be measured, and the realistic outcomes within a specific timeframe.

12. Question: Describe a process you use to align educational objectives with the overall curriculum and learning standards.

    Answer: I review the curriculum guidelines and learning standards set by the institute. Then, identify the core concepts and skills that need to be covered in my subject area. Formulate educational objectives that align with these standards and create a cohesive and comprehensive curriculum.

13. Question: How do you differentiate educational objectives to accommodate students with varying abilities and learning needs?

    Answer: formulate educational objectives with differentiated outcomes based on students' abilities and learning styles. Provide additional support or enrichment activities to ensure that all students can achieve the objectives at their level of proficiency.

14. Question: Explain how you communicate educational objectives to students and involve them in the learning process.

    Answer: present educational objectives to students at the beginning of each lesson or unit. Explain the purpose and relevance of the objectives and involve students in setting personal learning goals related to the broader educational objectives. This encourages ownership and engagement in their learning journey.

15. Question: How do you prioritize educational objectives to focus on the most critical concepts and skills for student learning?

Answer: prioritize educational objectives based on their significance in the overall learning process. Identify the foundational concepts and essential skills that serve as building blocks for future learning. This ensures that students master crucial content before moving on to more complex topics.

16. Question: Describe how you align educational objectives with assessment strategies to measure students' progress effectively.

Answer: design assessments that directly align with the educational objectives. This includes using different assessment types, such as formative assessments, quizzes, projects, and discussions, to gauge students' understanding and proficiency in relation to the objectives.

17. Question: How do you adapt and revise educational objectives when needed based on ongoing student assessment data?

Answer: regularly review student assessment data to identify areas of strength and areas that may need improvement. If necessary, modify the educational objectives, adjusting the scope or adding support as needed to ensure students' progress toward mastery.

18. Question: Explain how you integrate 21st-century skills, such as critical thinking, creativity, and collaboration, into your educational objectives.

Answer: include 21st-century skills as explicit components of the educational objectives. For example, an objective might state, "Students will collaborate in groups to solve real-world problems using critical thinking and creativity." This ensures that students develop essential skills for success in today's world.

19. Question: Describe a situation where you used backward design to formulate educational objectives for a specific unit or project.

Answer: In backward design, start by identifying the desired outcomes and then work backward to design learning experiences and assessments. For a science project, the educational objective might be, "Students will design and conduct experiments to demonstrate their understanding of the scientific method and data analysis."

20. Question: How do you use educational objectives to guide your lesson planning and instructional strategies?

Answer: Educational objectives serve as a roadmap for my lesson planning. They guide the selection of instructional strategies, learning activities, and resources to ensure that my teaching aligns with the desired learning outcomes.

Module 8: Students as a Source of Instructional Goals

These assessment questions and sample answers provide insights into how educators use instructional goals in the classroom. The answers should reflect the educators' ability to set clear and aligned goals, differentiate instruction, involve students in the learning process, and use goals to drive effective lesson planning and assessment

Below are assessment questions along with sample answers to evaluate educators' use of instructional goals in the classroom:

11. Question: How do you set clear and specific instructional goals for your lessons or units?

    Answer: set clear and specific instructional goals by identifying the key concepts and skills that I want my students to achieve. Use the SMART criteria to ensure that my goals are Specific, Measurable, Achievable, Relevant, and Time-bound.

12. Question: Describe how you align instructional goals with the overall curriculum and learning standards.

    Answer: align my instructional goals with the curriculum and learning standards, ensure that goals complement the larger scope of the curriculum.

13. Question: How do you differentiate instructional goals to meet the diverse learning needs and abilities of your students?

    Answer: I differentiate instructional goals by providing various learning pathways and activities to meet students' diverse needs. I adjust the level of complexity, offer additional support or extension activities, and tailor my teaching strategies accordingly.

14. Question: Explain how you communicate instructional goals to students and involve them in the learning process.

    Answer: clearly state instructional goals at the beginning of each lesson or unit, and share them with students. Involve students in the learning process by discussing the goals with them, encouraging questions, and seeking their input in setting personal learning targets.

15. Question: How do you prioritise instructional goals to focus on the most essential content and skills for student learning?

Answer: prioritise instructional goals by identifying the key concepts and skills that serve as foundational building blocks for further learning. Ensure that students master these essential components before moving on to more advanced topics.

16. Question: Describe how you align instructional goals with assessment strategies to measure students' progress effectively.

Answer: align instructional goals with various assessment strategies, such as quizzes, projects, and performance-based assessments. The assessments directly assess students' understanding of the content and skills related to the instructional goals.

17. Question: How do you adjust instructional goals based on ongoing student assessment data and their progress?

Answer: regularly review student assessment data to identify areas of strength and areas that may need additional support. If necessary, adjust instructional goals to better suit students' needs, ensuring that they are challenged appropriately.

18. Question: Explain how you incorporate real-life applications and relevance into instructional goals to enhance student engagement.

Answer: include real-life applications and relevance in my instructional goals by connecting the content to students' everyday lives. Use examples and scenarios that are relatable and demonstrate how the concepts and skills learned in the classroom are applicable in real-world situations.

19. Question: Describe a situation where you used backward design to develop instructional goals for a specific unit or project.

Answer: In backward design, start by identifying the desired learning outcomes and then plan the instructional strategies and activities to achieve those goals. For a history unit, the instructional goal might be, "Students will analyse primary sources to draw conclusions about historical events."

20. Question: How do you use instructional goals to guide your lesson planning and ensure a coherent and purposeful learning experience?

Answer: Instructional goals serve as the foundation of my lesson planning. They guide the selection of learning materials, teaching strategies, and classroom activities to ensure that each lesson aligns with the desired learning outcomes.

Module 9: Enhancing Student Learning

These assessment questions and sample answers provide insights into how educators enhance student learning in the classroom. The answers should reflect the educators' ability to create a positive and inclusive learning environment, use formative assessments to guide instruction, differentiate instruction, and promote active learning, critical thinking, and student autonomy

Below are assessment questions along with sample answers to evaluate educators' ability to enhance student learning in the classroom:

11. Question: How do you create a positive and inclusive learning environment that fosters student engagement and motivation?

    Answer: create a positive and inclusive learning environment by establishing clear expectations, promoting a culture of respect and collaboration, and valuing each student's unique contributions. Use a variety of teaching strategies and learning activities to keep students engaged and motivated to learn.

12. Question: Describe a situation where you used formative assessments to monitor student progress and adjust your teaching accordingly.

    Answer: During a project-based learning unit, the educator will show what was used during formative assessments like quizzes, observation, and student reflections to gauge students' understanding and progress. Based on the results, how they adjusted the teaching approach, providing additional support to struggling students and extension opportunities for those who excelled.

13. Question: How do you differentiate instruction to meet the diverse learning needs and abilities of your students?

    Answer: differentiate instruction by providing various learning opportunities, tailored to individual students' needs and abilities. Use flexible grouping, offer additional support or enrichment activities, and provide varied learning resources to ensure that all students can access and engage with the content.

14. Question: Explain how you incorporate real-world connections and examples into your lessons to make learning relevant and meaningful for students.

    Answer: I incorporate real-world connections by using current events, case studies, and relevant examples that relate to students' lives. By showing the practical applications of the concepts learned in class, students understand the relevance of their learning and are more motivated to engage.

15. Question: How do you encourage active learning and critical thinking in the classroom?

    Answer: encourage active learning and critical thinking by using interactive teaching methods such as group discussions, debates, problem-solving activities, and hands-on experiments. Ask thought-provoking questions that require students to analyse and evaluate information to develop their critical thinking skills.

16. Question: Describe how you provide timely and constructive feedback to students to support their learning and growth.

    Answer: provide timely and constructive feedback through written comments on assignments, one-on-one discussions, and in-class feedback sessions. Focus on highlighting strengths, providing specific suggestions for improvement, and encouraging students to reflect on their progress.

17. Question: How do you promote a growth mind-set in your classroom to inspire students to embrace challenges and view failures as opportunities for learning?

    Answer: promote a growth mind-set by praising effort and perseverance rather than just outcomes. Encourage students to view mistakes as valuable learning experiences and emphasize the power of "yet" - acknowledging that they may not have mastered something yet, but they can improve with dedication and practice.

18. Question: Explain how you integrate technology and digital resources to enhance student learning experiences.

    Answer: integrate technology by using interactive whiteboards, educational apps, online simulations, and multimedia resources. These tools enhance students' understanding, provide opportunities for self-paced learning, and enable them to explore concepts in a dynamic and engaging way.

19. Question: Describe a strategy you use to foster a sense of ownership and autonomy in students' learning journeys.

    Answer: encourage student autonomy by offering choice in assignments and projects, allowing them to pursue topics of personal interest, and involving them in setting goals and evaluating their progress. This fosters a sense of ownership and responsibility for their learning.

20. Question: How do you promote collaboration and peer learning among students to enhance their overall learning experience?

Answer: promote collaboration through group projects, collaborative discussions, and peer feedback activities. By working together, students learn from one another, develop teamwork skills, and gain diverse perspectives on the subject matter.

ISBN: 9798872216605

Module 10: Creating Bridges between Goals and Experiences

These assessment questions and sample answers provide insights into how educators create bridges between learning goals and students' experiences in the classroom. The answers should reflect the educators' ability to connect learning objectives to real-life experiences, scaffold learning, promote student autonomy, and use formative assessments to track progress and adjust instruction accordingly.

Below are assessment questions along with sample answers to evaluate educators' ability to create bridges between goals and experiences in the classroom:

11. Question: How do you connect the learning goals and objectives to real-life experiences and prior knowledge of students?

      Answer: I connect learning goals to real-life experiences by using relatable examples, case studies, and scenarios that are relevant to students' lives. I also tap into their prior knowledge and experiences to build connections and make new concepts more accessible.

12. Question: Describe a specific lesson where you used experiential learning to bridge the gap between learning goals and students' experiences.

      Answer: The answer must show the activity, the action and the outcome for example "During a science lesson about the water cycle,/ they took students outside to observe the weather and gather data. / This hands-on experience helped them connect theoretical concepts to real-life observations, making the learning more meaningful and memorable".

13. Question: How do you ensure that students understand the purpose and relevance of the learning goals in relation to their future academic and personal growth?

      Answer: explain the significance of learning goals by discussing their relevance to students' future academic pursuits and real-world applications. I also emphasize the lifelong learning skills they develop through achieving these goals, which will benefit them beyond the classroom.

14. Question: Explain how you scaffold learning experiences to support students in reaching their learning goals step-by-step.

      Answer: scaffold learning experiences by breaking down complex concepts into manageable steps. Provide additional resources and support as needed, gradually removing scaffolding as students gain confidence and proficiency.

15. Question: How do you incorporate interdisciplinary connections to create bridges between different subjects and learning goals?

    Answer: incorporate interdisciplinary connections by integrating concepts from different subjects. For example, during a history lesson, they might include relevant literature or art to provide a more comprehensive understanding of the topic.

16. Question: Describe a strategy you use to encourage students to set personal learning goals that align with the broader learning objectives.

    Answer: encourage students to set personal learning goals by having them reflect on their strengths, areas for improvement, and interests. Guide them in aligning these goals with the broader learning objectives and developing action plans to achieve them.

17. Question: How do you promote self-directed learning and independent thinking to bridge the gap between goals and students' own experiences?

    Answer: promote self-directed learning by providing opportunities for student choice, encouraging inquiry-based projects, and guiding them to seek answers independently. This approach fosters critical thinking and empowers students to take ownership of their learning journey.

18. Question: Explain how you use formative assessments to track students' progress and adjust learning experiences to better align with their needs.

    Answer: use formative assessments such as quizzes, discussions, and observations to gauge students' understanding and progress toward the learning goals. Based on the results, adjust instruction and learning experiences to meet individual needs.

19. Question: Describe a specific activity where you used technology to bridge the gap between learning goals and students' experiences.

    Answer: During a language arts lesson, for example the "incorporated interactive online storytelling tools that allowed students to create and share their narratives digitally. This technology-enabled students to express themselves creatively while achieving language arts learning objectives".

20. Question: How do you encourage students to reflect on their learning experiences and make connections between their achievements and the broader learning goals?

Answer: encourage students to reflect on their learning experiences through journals, discussions, and self-assessments. During these reflections, students are prompted to identify how their achievements align with the broader learning goals and articulate the progress they have made.

Module 11: Diploma Educators "Teaching Skills" - Second Assessment

Module 12: Behaviour and Goals as Motivation Sources

These assessment questions and sample answers provide insights into how educators use behaviour and goals as motivation sources in the classroom. The answers should reflect the educators' ability to implement positive reinforcement, goal setting, intrinsic motivation techniques, behaviour management, and progress monitoring to create a supportive and motivating learning environment.

11. Question: How do you use positive reinforcement and rewards to motivate students towards achieving their learning goals?

     Answer: use positive reinforcement by acknowledging and praising students' efforts and achievements. For example, they might offer verbal praise, stickers, or small rewards for completing tasks or making progress toward their learning goals.

12. Question: Describe a situation where you effectively used goal setting to motivate students to excel in their academic performance.

     Answer: Give an example with the activity, the action and the outcome for example "At the beginning of the semester, I worked with students to set specific, achievable academic goals for themselves. Throughout the term, we revisited these goals, and students were motivated to excel as they saw their progress and how it aligned with their aspirations".

13. Question: How do you create a supportive classroom culture that encourages students to take ownership of their learning and set personal growth goals?

     Answer: create a supportive classroom culture by fostering a growth mind-set and encouraging students to set personal growth goals aligned with their interests and aspirations. I provide resources and support to help them achieve these goals and celebrate their progress along the way.

14. Question: Explain how you use behaviour management strategies to address challenging behaviours and maintain a positive learning environment.

                 Answer: behaviour management strategies such as clear expectations, consistent consequences, and positive reinforcement are used to address challenging behaviours. By maintaining a positive and respectful learning environment, it can help students stay motivated and engaged in their learning.

15. Question: Describe a specific technique you use to promote intrinsic motivation among students.

Answer: use inquiry-based learning and choice-based assignments to promote intrinsic motivation. By allowing students to explore topics of interest and take ownership of their learning, they become more engaged and self-motivated to excel.

16. Question: How do you provide opportunities for students to reflect on their progress and celebrate their achievements?

Answer: provide regular opportunities for students to reflect on their learning journey through self-assessment and discussions. We celebrate their achievements, both big and small, during class activities, parent-teacher conferences, and end-of-term events.

17. Question: How do you use goal progress monitoring to track students' development and offer guidance to those who may be struggling?

Answer: use goal progress monitoring through regular formative assessments and individual check-ins. For example if a student is struggling, offer personalized support, additional resources, or revision opportunities to help them get back on track.

18. Question: Describe a strategy you use to help students see the connection between their efforts and their academic achievements.

Answer: use data tracking and progress charts to visually demonstrate to students how their efforts contribute to their academic achievements. This helps to understand the cause-and-effect relationship between their dedication and success.

19. Question: How do you encourage students to set both short-term and long-term goals to sustain their motivation throughout the academic year?

Answer: I encourage students to set short-term goals to maintain focus and momentum in their learning, as well as long-term goals to envision their academic progress and achievements over time. We regularly review and adjust these goals together.

20. Question: Explain how you promote a growth mind-set in your classroom to inspire students to embrace challenges and persevere in their learning.

Answer: promote a growth mind-set by celebrating effort and resilience in the face of challenges. Use stories of successful individuals who overcame obstacles through perseverance, fostering a culture where students view challenges as opportunities for growth.

Module 13: Motivation Related to Attributions and Interests
These assessment questions and sample answers provide insights into how educators address motivation related to attributions and interests in the classroom. The answers should reflect the educators' ability to foster a growth mind-set, leverage students' interests, provide choices and challenges, offer meaningful feedback, and create a supportive learning environment that promotes intrinsic motivation

Below are assessment questions along with sample answers to evaluate educators' ability to understand and address motivation related to attributions and interests in the classroom:

11. Question: How do you foster a growth mind-set among your students to encourage them to see challenges as opportunities for learning and growth?

    Answer: foster a growth mind-set by praising students' efforts and highlighting their progress. Encourage them to embrace challenges and view mistakes as part of the learning process, reinforcing the belief that their abilities can be developed through dedication and hard work.

12. Question: Describe a situation where you helped a student overcome a negative attribution or self-perception about their academic abilities.

    Answer: Give an example, (activity, action, result) "a student who believed they were (activity) not good at math due to previous struggles. They provided (action) extra support, individualized feedback, and opportunities for success. As (result) they experienced progress and success, their negative attribution transformed into a more positive perception of their abilities".

13. Question: How do you leverage students' interests and passions to enhance their motivation and engagement in the learning process?

    Answer: incorporate students' interests into lesson planning and offer opportunities for them to explore topics related to their passions. This personalization fosters greater engagement and enthusiasm for learning.

14. Question: Explain how you provide choices and autonomy in learning activities to increase students' intrinsic motivation.

    Answer: offer students choices in assignments, projects, and learning pathways. This empowers them to take ownership of their learning, increasing their intrinsic motivation as they engage in activities that align with their interests and preferences.

15. Question: Describe a strategy you use to help students set meaningful learning goals that are connected to their interests and aspirations.

Answer: I facilitate goal-setting sessions where students reflect on their interests and aspirations. We collaboratively set learning goals that align with their passions, making the objectives personally meaningful and motivating.

16. Question: How do you use positive feedback and recognition to reinforce students' efforts and accomplishments in the classroom?

Answer: use positive feedback to acknowledge students' efforts, improvement, and achievements. Celebrate their successes publicly, recognizing their hard work and perseverance to further motivate them.

17. Question: Explain how you provide challenges and opportunities for success to cater to the varying levels of student ability and interests.

Answer: differentiate instruction by offering various levels of challenges and learning opportunities based on individual abilities and interests. This ensures that all students are appropriately challenged and can experience success in their learning journey.

18. Question: Describe a situation where you helped a student develop a sense of competence and self-efficacy in a subject they initially found challenging.

Answer: Give an example (activity, action, result) I had a student struggling with writing who lacked confidence. Through targeted support, encouraging feedback, and gradual skill-building, the student's confidence and competence in writing improved significantly.

19. Question: How do you create a positive and supportive classroom culture where students feel comfortable taking academic risks and trying new approaches to learning?

Answer: establish a safe and respectful environment where mistakes are seen as opportunities for growth. Encourage collaboration, peer support, and a willingness to try new approaches to foster a culture of learning and exploration.

20. Question: Explain how you address students' individual interests within the constraints of the curriculum to keep them engaged and motivated.

Answer: use creative lesson planning and instructional techniques to infuse students' interests into the curriculum. By finding connections between their passions and the required content, it is easy to keep them engaged and motivated throughout the learning process.

Module 14: Self Efficacy

These assessment questions and sample answers provide insights into how educators support self-efficacy in the classroom. The answers should reflect the educators' ability to promote self-belief, use goal setting and feedback to support personal growth, create a supportive learning environment, and foster a growth mind-set that emphasizes effort and resilience.

Below are assessment questions along with sample answers to evaluate educators' ability to understand and support self-efficacy in the classroom:

11. Question: How do you promote a sense of self-efficacy among your students to believe in their ability to succeed academically?

    Answer: promote self-efficacy by providing opportunities for students to experience success and acknowledging their achievements. Offer encouragement and support, emphasizing that with effort and perseverance; they can overcome challenges and excel in their academic endeavours.

12. Question: Describe a situation where you helped a student develop a stronger sense of self-efficacy in a subject they previously found challenging.

    Answer: Give example (activity, action, result) "I had a student struggling in mathematics who lacked confidence. I provided targeted support, scaffolded learning experiences, and praised their efforts and progress. As their confidence grew, their belief in their mathematical abilities improved, leading to greater success.

13. Question: How do you use goal setting and individualized learning plans to support students' self-efficacy and personal growth?

    Answer: involve students in setting realistic and achievable goals. Collaborate with them to develop individualized learning plans that align with their interests and strengths. This fosters a sense of ownership and empowerment, increasing their self-efficacy.

14. Question: Explain how you use positive affirmations and constructive feedback to nurture students' self-belief and confidence.

    Answer: use positive affirmations to remind students of their strengths and capabilities. Additionally, provide constructive feedback that highlights their progress and offers specific suggestions for improvement, helping them build on their strengths.

15. Question: Describe a strategy you use to help students overcome self-doubt and fear of failure.

Answer: Give example (activity, action, result) "engage students in discussions about resilience and growth mind-set. Share stories of individuals who faced challenges and turned failures into learning opportunities, encouraging students to view setbacks as a natural part of the learning process".

16. Question: How do you create a supportive classroom environment where students feel comfortable taking academic risks and trying new approaches to learning?

Answer: create a safe and non-judgmental space where students are encouraged to share their ideas and opinions. Foster a culture that values effort and improvement, ensuring that students feel comfortable taking risks in their learning journey.

17. Question: Explain how you use differentiation and flexible grouping to address individual learning needs and build students' confidence.

Answer: differentiate instruction to meet students at their current level of understanding and gradually challenge them to grow. I use flexible grouping to offer additional support or extension opportunities, allowing students to work at a pace that builds their confidence.

18. Question: Describe a situation where you helped a student overcome academic setbacks and maintain a positive outlook on their abilities.

Answer: Give example (activity, action, result) "I worked with a student who experienced a significant academic setback due to an extended absence. I provided personalized catch-up sessions, emphasized their progress, and celebrated their efforts. This helped the student regain confidence and motivation".

19. Question: How do you foster a growth mind-set and emphasize the role of effort and perseverance in achieving success?

Answer: I foster a growth mind-set by highlighting the value of effort and hard work. I encourage students to embrace challenges, learn from mistakes, and believe that their abilities can be developed through dedication and practice.

20. Question: Explain how you celebrate students' achievements and growth to reinforce their self-efficacy and boost their confidence.

Answer: celebrate students' achievements through verbal praise, recognition in front of peers, and acknowledgment in school newsletters or assemblies.

Celebrating progress and growth reinforces their belief in themselves and motivates them to continue striving for success.

Module 15: Self-Determination

These assessment questions and sample answers provide insights into how educators support self-determination in the classroom. The answers should reflect the educators' ability to encourage student autonomy, support goal-setting and self-reflection, foster a positive classroom culture, provide relevant learning experiences, and recognize and celebrate students' strengths and talents to enhance their self-determination.

Below are assessment questions along with sample answers to evaluate educators' ability to understand and support self-determination in the classroom:

11. Question: How do you encourage student autonomy and choice in the learning process to foster self-determination?

Answer: Encourage student autonomy by offering choices in assignments, projects, and learning activities. Involve students in decision-making and allow them to pursue topics of personal interest within the curriculum.

12. Question: Describe a situation where you helped a student develop a stronger sense of self-determination and ownership over their learning.

Answer: Give example (activity, action, result) "I had a student who initially lacked motivation in a particular subject. By engaging them in a project where they could explore their passions and make choices about their learning, their sense of ownership and determination increased, leading to improved engagement and performance."

13. Question: How do you support students in setting and working towards self-determined goals that align with their interests and aspirations?

Answer: Support students in setting self-determined goals by helping them identify their interests and passions. We work together to create personalized learning plans that connect with their aspirations and provide opportunities for growth.

14. Question: Explain how you use self-reflection and goal-setting activities to develop students' self-awareness and enhance their self-determination.

Answer: Incorporate self-reflection activities where students assess their strengths, challenges, and progress. We use this information to set meaningful goals and track their growth over time, enhancing their self-awareness and self-determination.

15. Question: Describe a strategy you use to help students overcome obstacles and develop a sense of agency in their academic pursuits.

	Answer:	Encourage students to view obstacles as opportunities for problem-solving and growth. By providing support and guidance, it helps them develop the confidence to take initiative and find solutions to challenges they encounter.
16.	Question:	How do you foster a classroom culture that values and celebrates individual student contributions and voices?
	Answer:	Foster a classroom culture that values individual contributions by creating a supportive and respectful environment. Actively listen to students' ideas and perspectives, encouraging open dialogue and valuing diverse viewpoints.
17.	Question:	Explain how you use authentic and relevant learning experiences to promote students' intrinsic motivation and self-determination.
	Answer:	Design learning experiences that are connected to real-life applications and relevant to students' interests. By demonstrating the practicality and significance of what they are learning, students become more motivated and self-determined in their studies.
18.	Question:	Describe a situation where you used collaborative learning activities to foster a sense of empowerment and collective responsibility among students.
	Answer:	Give example (activity, action result) group projects where students had to collaborate, share ideas, and make collective decisions. This fostered a sense of empowerment and collective responsibility, as they saw the impact of their collaborative efforts.
19.	Question:	How do you provide opportunities for students to develop and showcase their talents and strengths, fostering self-determination in their learning journey?
	Answer:	Provide platforms for students to showcase their talents and strengths through presentations, performances, and projects. This recognition and celebration of their unique abilities boost their confidence and self-determination.
20.	Question:	Explain how you adapt your teaching approach to accommodate students' interests and learning preferences, promoting their sense of autonomy and self-determination.
	Answer:	Adapt my teaching approach by offering various learning options and resources to cater to students' diverse interests and learning styles. This

approach allows students to make choices that align with their preferences, fostering a greater sense of autonomy and self-determination.

ISBN: 9798872216605   A.M. McIlwraith. FAIBHS., D.S.Ch.   Page 211

Module 16: Combining Motivation Theories

These assessment questions and sample answers provide insights into how educators effectively combine motivation theories in the classroom. The answers should reflect the educators' ability to design engaging and motivating learning experiences, leverage a variety of motivational theories, and foster a positive and supportive learning environment that addresses students' needs and aspirations

Below are assessment questions along with sample answers to evaluate educators' ability to effectively combine motivation theories in the classroom:

11. Question: How do you incorporate aspects of both intrinsic and extrinsic motivation in your teaching to engage and inspire students?

       Answer: combine intrinsic and extrinsic motivation by designing learning experiences that appeal to students' interests and curiosity (intrinsic) while providing recognition, rewards, or positive feedback for their efforts (extrinsic). This approach ensures a well-rounded motivational environment.

12. Question: Describe a lesson where you used self-determination theory to empower students to take ownership of their learning.

       Answer: give an example (activity, action, result) in a project-based learning activity, students could choose their topics and plan their project steps. By providing autonomy and relatedness (collaboration with peers), it empowered them to take ownership of their learning, fostering intrinsic motivation.

13. Question: How do you incorporate elements of both goal-setting theory and expectancy theory to enhance students' motivation and performance?

       Answer: use goal-setting theory to help students set specific, challenging, and achievable learning objectives. Simultaneously, apply expectancy theory by providing clear instructions, demonstrating the connection between effort and success, and offering support to build students' confidence in achieving their goals.

14. Question: Explain how you utilize positive reinforcement from behaviourism and cognitive evaluation theory to create a positive and motivating classroom atmosphere.

       Answer: use positive reinforcement to acknowledge and celebrate students' achievements and efforts (behaviourism). Apply cognitive evaluation theory by promoting autonomy and a growth mind-set, encouraging students to view challenges as opportunities for learning and growth.

15. Question: Describe a strategy you use to leverage elements of the hierarchy of needs theory and self-determination theory to meet students' psychological and emotional needs.

     Answer: create a safe and supportive classroom environment that fulfils students' psychological needs for belonging and relatedness. By offering opportunities for autonomy and competence, it addresses their self-determination needs, ensuring a motivating learning environment.

16. Question: How do you integrate elements of the cognitive theory of motivation and the attribution theory to help students develop a positive outlook on their abilities and effort?

     Answer: use cognitive theory to teach students about the power of positive self-talk and mind-set. Concurrently, employ attribution theory by encouraging students to attribute their successes to effort and strategy, rather than fixed abilities.

17. Question: Explain how you use elements of both the expectancy-value theory and the equity theory to maintain a fair and motivating classroom atmosphere.

     Answer: use the expectancy-value theory by helping students understand the relevance and value of their learning. Apply the equity theory by ensuring fairness and equal opportunities for participation, acknowledging individual efforts, and providing support when needed.

18. Question: Describe a lesson where you integrated elements of the self-efficacy theory and the achievement goal theory to boost students' confidence and willingness to tackle challenging tasks.

     Answer: During a problem-solving activity, emphasized students' past successes (self-efficacy) and set learning goals focused on mastery and improvement (achievement goal theory). This combination motivated students to approach challenges with confidence and a growth mind-set.

19. Question: How do you balance between intrinsic interest and extrinsic rewards when designing learning experiences to maintain students' long-term motivation?

     Answer: ensure that learning experiences are inherently interesting and relevant to students' lives (intrinsic interest). Occasionally offer extrinsic rewards or recognition to celebrate their accomplishments and maintain enthusiasm for continuous learning.

20. Question: Explain how you use elements of reinforcement theory and goal-setting theory to create a positive feedback loop that reinforces students' progress and effort.

Answer: To provide frequent positive feedback and reinforcement to acknowledge students' progress and effort (reinforcement theory). Simultaneously, use goal-setting theory by collaboratively setting new learning objectives based on their achievements, fostering a sense of continuous growth and accomplishment.

Printed in Great Britain
by Amazon

35952054R00119